"In *Feminine Registers*, Jennifer Copeland manages to transcend essentialist models of gender to create a deeply relational and communicative approach to feminist preaching. Copeland situates gender in the midst of complex relationships and expectations within communities and asks how the 'field' (content/context), 'tone' (roles and relationships), and 'mode' (embodiment, implementation), conspire together to create a distinctively feminist 'register.' This promises to become one of a handful of important books on feminist homiletical method."

—JOHN S. MCCLURE
Charles G. Finney Professor of Preaching and Worship, Vanderbilt Divinity School

"*Feminine Registers* is a wake-up call to homiletics. Drawing on feminist theory and the linguistic concept of register, Jennifer Copeland provides a thick analysis of the often-ignored role gender plays in preaching. Along the way, through homiletical reflection and practical examples, Copeland demonstrates the ways in which women's voices enrich the church's proclamation. This book is an important contribution to the homiletical literature and a valuable gift to both teachers and preachers."

—CHARLES CAMPBELL
Professor of Homiletics, Duke Divinity School

Feminine Registers

Feminine Registers

The Importance of Women's Voices for Christian Preaching

Jennifer E. Copeland

CASCADE *Books* • Eugene, Oregon

FEMININE REGISTERS
The Importance of Women's Voices for Christian Preaching

Copyright © 2014 Jennifer E. Copeland. All rights reserved. Except for brief quotations in critical publications or reviews, no part of this book may be reproduced in any manner without prior written permission from the publisher. Write: Permissions, Wipf and Stock Publishers, 199 W. 8th Ave., Suite 3, Eugene, OR 97401.

Cascade Books
An Imprint of Wipf and Stock Publishers
199 W. 8th Ave., Suite 3
Eugene, OR 97401

www.wipfandstock.com

ISBN 13: 978-1-62564-219-6

Cataloguing-in-Publication data:

Copeland, Jennifer E.

Feminine registers : the importance of women's voices for Christian preaching / Jennifer E. Copeland.

xviii + 150 pp. ; 23 cm. Includes bibliographical references and index(es).

ISBN 13: 978-1-62564-219-6

1. Feminist theology. 2. Preaching. 3. Women in Christianity—United States. I. Title.

BV4211.3 .C59 2014

Manufactured in the U.S.A.

Scripture quotations are from New Revised Standard Version, copyright © 1989, Division of Christian Education of the National Council of Churches of the Christ in the U.S.A. Used by permission. All rights reserved.

For my parents, Posey and Sarah Copeland

Contents

Acknowledgments   ix

Introduction   xi

1 Women Then—How We Got Here   1

2 Women Now—The Current Situation   25

3 What, Who, and How—The Real Meaning   48

4 Sermon Registers at Work   75

5 Listening for the Register   95

6 A New Register   122

Bibliography   135

Name and Subject Index   141

Scripture Index   149

Acknowledgments

Books are only as good as all the people who help write them. Richard Lischer helped the most with this book, reading the manuscript so many times he might know more about it than I do. Coffee and cobbler enhanced the process. Teresa Berger and Mary McClintock Fulkerson further spiced up the book while we spiced our palates with good food and good wine. There were students along the way who read sections and commented on them, colleagues who heard ideas and improved upon them, friends who took long walks and listened to the latest challenge, and family members who offered a different kind of encouragement without ever reading a word. Special thanks to my parents, who have always believed I could do what I said I would do, even when neither they nor I could see how it would all work out. I hope I have passed along that same hopeful vision to my children, Nathan and Hannah, as they stand on the cusp of becoming adults.

Introduction

The voices of feminist theory have been increasingly acknowledged in the fields of theology and ethics, historical studies, and biblical hermeneutics. Paradoxically, those voices are not as clearly heard in the homiletical arena, the area of the church most heavily invested in speaking out loud. The dimensions of feminist theory that have been examined within homiletics focus primarily on physical or social differences between male and female preachers with an emphasis on their advantages and disadvantages.[1] For instance, men have lower voices that carry better in a crowded room or women have nurturing personalities that are more relational, both assumptions that rely more on gender stereotypes than they do on reality. Likewise, the role of biblical interpretation for authorizing conventional traditions and the use of theological grammar to perpetuate an androcentric climate have received more attention in recent years. Attempts to redress each of these matters are valuable and necessary conversations toward a fuller appreciation of God's word.

What has yet to be critically examined, however, is the constellation of meanings influenced by gender-related issues of authority and self-disclosure in the act of preaching. Implied subject positions are locked into implied meanings, but when the roles change the meanings begin to shift. The challenge, then, is to offer a gender analysis of preaching without reverting to essentialist claims about those who self-identify as men or women.[2] Establishing this difference involves understanding gender roles as they are both adopted by us and projected upon us. In doing so we can begin to claim the distinctiveness of women's voices for Christian preaching.

---

1. For previous material related to women as preachers in the North American context, see Carroll, *Women of the Cloth*; Ice, *Clergy Women and Their Worldviews*; Noren, *The Woman in the Pulpit*; McGee, *Wresting with the Patriarchs*; and Kim, *Women Preaching*.

2. Gender, of course, does not divide neatly into two categories, nor are the categories into which it divides necessarily fixed. See Butler, *Gender Trouble*; Fausto-Sterling, *Sexing the Body*.

Introduction

It should be noted that over the past few decades a great deal of scholarship in the field of gender studies has focused on the inadequacy of sexual dimorphism when thinking about gender and human sexuality. Researchers point out that our views about sexuality, ranging from physical appearance to brain function to biological hormones, have largely been shaped by cultural beliefs that present only two choices. Sex categories and sexual behavior, first under the purview of religious and civil authorities, moved to the arena of the scientific and medical communities without any noticeable shift away from a dichotomous view of human sexuality. Indeed, the recommendation by the American Association of Pediatricians for infants born with ambiguous genitalia remains, "all individuals should receive a gender assignment."[3] Recognizing that several scholars now challenge the assumptions of sexual dimorphism and provide more accurate definitions of human sexuality along a spectrum, it remains the case that most people continue to think of sexual differentiation as male and female. While acknowledging these categories are inadequate, for the purposes of this study, I will employ the terms *man* and *woman*, *male* and *female* to indicate persons who "self-identify" as such and who are identified by others as such.

Likewise, the preachers and the homiletical systems examined here are only a small slice of the rich diversity possible for proclaiming the word of God. No attempt is being made to include the myriad of preaching styles that might be differentiated by race, class, or denomination. Instead, this analysis relies on those traditions—largely white, middle-class, and mainline—that have produced a substantial body of homiletical literature in the hope a close study of this literature and the genre of preaching associated with it might inform those who teach and preach in other settings.

While the definition of "preaching" has been expanded by some feminist scholars to include the work and witness of women outside the typical boundaries of the church and the testimony of women outside the conventional borders of a worshiping congregation, this book will concentrate on the articulated voices of women in the congregation gathered for worship. Within this setting, issues of gender affect the content of the sermon at several levels. To begin with, the assumptions in the community about women will shape the meaning-making possibilities for the content of her sermon.

---

3. Though surgical correction of ambiguous genitalia within "twenty-four hours" is no longer recommended by the American Association of Pediatricians, it is still clearly their policy to assign gender to each human being using the dimorphous categories of male/female. See Lee et al., "Consensus Statement on Management of Intersex Disorders."

Introduction

Subsequently, the preacher may selectively tailor her words to meet the gendered assumptions and expectations of the congregation.

Even though most preaching implies one person speaking to a congregation of listeners, preaching is not a one-directional flow of information from the pulpit to the pew. The preacher does not dispense the meaning of a text from the pulpit, even if the sermon seems to start from that location. Meaning comes through the relationship of the text with a particular community of listeners whose hearing is determined by their historical and cultural conditions. The word of God may still be constant, but the significance of that word for the lives of those who receive it will have as many different possibilities as there are recipients. Individuals listening to a sermon participate in the production of that sermon through the discursive processes forming their existence—that is, their political, economic, societal, cultural, and, perhaps most importantly, religious surroundings.

Besides the obvious ingredient of content, the meaning-making possibilities for a sermon also include the relationship between the communicating parties—congregation and preacher—and the medium of the communication. Each of these variables must be considered in order to provide a thicker analysis of gender issues within the church and gender roles for preachers. By utilizing the linguistic concept of register,[4] this book will suggest an analysis of preaching that recognizes the theological and semantic contributions of women, but then moves beyond these categories to examine how gender influences these meanings.

Register can help us analyze how the voices of women are enriching the discursive possibilities for the proclamation of the word. Each of the register variables—field, tenor, and mode—is impacted in different ways when a woman delivers the sermon. Since changing just one variable can alter the entire meaning of the communication, changing two or more variables will certainly provide new ways of hearing the word. Register variables are explained the following ways:

- Field—what and where? The subject of a sermon is predetermined by a host of variables, scripture being dominant among them, but even the biblical translation and commentaries used for exegetical study will influence how content is used in a particular context. Beyond

---

4. First developed by M. A. K. Halliday, *Language as Social Semiotic*, and further refined by John Frow, *Marxism and Literary History*, the concept of register offers an analytical tool for understanding how meaning extends beyond, and sometimes in spite of, the words that are spoken aloud.

Introduction

scripture, there are a variety of sermon components selected by the preacher such as allegory and metaphor, irony and sarcasm, or illustrations and examples. Choices made by the preacher will dictate much about the meaning of the sermon. Furthermore, the experiences of women should be interpreted from within their "situated knowledge."[5] In particular, situated on the margins of power in the church, women occupy a position from which they can consider the center differently from those firmly entrenched in it. At the same time they continue to maintain a constructive understanding of a margin that is virtually unknown by those in the center. Such a critical analysis of the center by those not inured to its advantages offers the possibility of new and different interpretations of God's reign in the world.

- Tenor—who? The relationship between the communicating parties affects meanings. Simply recognizing that more women are in church than men[6] initiates a diagnosis of how their majority presence influences the relationship between the preacher and the congregation in particular ways. Beyond this, the way history is recited and our assumptions about relational categories within history offer particular conventions that govern our understandings of one another. These conventions influence the meaning of the communication that occurs.

- Mode—how? When considering how the preacher communicates, it is important to consider whether there is a distinctly feminine mode and, if so, how such a mode might responsibly be described. Specifically, where do women resist and reinterpret the status quo proclamation of many pulpits? Is such resistance viable within current cultural norms of communication? To begin answering these questions, we must consider the physical body and the gendered perceptions of the body that are projected upon women preachers.

Field, tenor, and mode are not components of speech, but rather determinants, collectively serving to shape meaning. The communication occurs at the intersection of all three—field, tenor, and mode—governed by a conceptual framework that determines the production, transmission, and reception of appropriate meanings. A great deal can be said about how

---

5. Donna Haraway uses this phrase to define objectivity as the place where one's perspective originates. "Feminist objectivity is about limited location and situated knowledge, not about transcendence and splitting of subject and object" ("Situated Knowledges," 190).

6. Braude, "Women's History *Is* American Religious History."

Introduction

register operates in the preaching event. The appropriation of meanings will depend on how these variables relate to one another. Changing one variable—the gender of the person in the pulpit—might shift the register slightly, or it might change the meaning altogether. In each case, the meaning brought to a sermon has important implications for the transmission of the word.

To lay the foundation for examining these meaning-making possibilities within preaching, we must also consider the authority of women to speak within the biblical and ecclesial traditions. Feminist scholars in both the fields of biblical studies and historical theology provide ample commentary on the scripting of women by these respective traditions, yet few preachers consider that some parts of the ecclesial tradition have been selectively retained while others are conveniently forgotten in order to legitimate particular gender preferences. Likewise, the biblical tradition is replete with textual biases,[7] mistranslations,[8] and misinterpretations.[9] A close inspection of the biblical and ecclesial traditions reveals a persistent pattern of submission and subordination of women to men. This becomes a tool for the continued submission of women to men and validates the subordination of women within the church. Compounding the paucity of female agency in scripture, the lectionary, used by many of the world's Christians, excludes most of the stories about women found in the Bible.[10] Each of these claims is well documented by numerous scholars; however, they are important ingredients for recognizing and understanding the preconceptions associated with women who preach. Furthermore, as more women have enrolled in seminary over the past few decades, the leading homiletical textbooks used by these seminaries have paid little attention to the theological and semantic contributions of women to the proclamation of the word. In response, Rebecca Chopp argues in *The Power to Speak* that

---

7. Out of more than three hundred recorded prayers or allusions to prayer in scripture, less than ten come from women (cf. Berger, "Contemporary Church and the Real Presence of Women").

8. E.g., Junia translated as Junias, a mistranslation that continues to persist, as evidenced by a 2004 publication titled *All the Women of the Bible* that does not include Junia.

9. E.g., Mary Magdalene commonly referred to as a prostitute.

10. The book of Ruth appears on two consecutive Sundays in Year B as the Old Testament lection. Meanwhile, the Samuel books run for twelve consecutive Sundays in Year B, with a few guest appearances on other Sundays and in other years. One could argue that these books are longer, but that only strengthens the claim that scripture contains more material about men.

Introduction

women's voices are crucial for inculcating a deeper and fuller understanding of the "Word as perfectly open sign." Chopp defines this:

> As the perfectly open sign we may say what the Word is, in our best approximation, but also how it sustains the process of speaking. Here the Word is not that which breaks into discourse, or one that governs it, rather it is the full inclusivity of discourse; it creates and restores speech, it both allows symbols to have meaning and pushes against any fixed meanings.[11]

Five scholars in the arena of homiletics and preaching provide valuable entry points for examining these themes. Christine Smith is one of the first homiletical scholars to produce a distinctly feminist homiletic, and her work has consistently employed feminist themes for nearly two decades. Lucy Lind Hogan and Anna Carter Florence represent two scholars who have built upon the work of Smith but who have reached somewhat different conclusions. Mary Catherine Hilkert, a Roman Catholic Dominican, shares some similarities with Hogan and Florence, but her location in a tradition that denies ordination to women lends a different perspective to her homiletical suggestions precisely because she does not assume that women can be heard. John McClure does not self-identify as a feminist scholar, but rather offers a poststructural approach to homiletics. Because poststructuralism has provided fertile ground for feminist theory to take root and flourish, McClure's approach informs the task at hand. Understanding these academic techniques shows how the register variables provide different meaning-making possibilities for each scholar and thus for any preacher.[12]

Finally, based on this analysis we can begin to create a new preaching register more resonant to the particular meanings that women bring to the preaching event. Stories are imprinted on our minds before we are cognizant of their power, and sermons are an integral part of this process. How we come to know God and the language we use to communicate this knowledge shape our perceptions of the world and our behavior toward one another. Recognizing and celebrating the very different contributions made by women and men as preachers will expand the homiletical possibilities

---

11. Chopp, *Power to Speak*, 31.

12. All of the sermons utilized for this analysis are in manuscript form. Though I have seen and heard several other sermons by a few of these preachers, I have not seen or heard all of them preach. In order to approximate similarity for the analysis, I opted for a consistent medium between each of them.

Introduction

for the church's proclamation. The ways in which a preacher gives presence to these matters through the sermon will do more to change perceptions about gender ideology than all the sermons crafted to address women's issues and all the special Sundays designated for women to preach. The goal of a feminist homiletic is not merely to include women "in the company of preachers," but to craft a new register for the preaching event.

1

Women Then—How We Got Here

"Preach if you must, but don't call it that!"[1]

From the moment Mary Magdalene proclaimed, "I have seen the Lord," women have been preaching the gospel. More often than not, as John Wesley intoned to Sarah Crosby, they have not called it that. The struggle over whether women might legitimately and authoritatively preach the gospel begins with the first proclamation of the resurrection and continues into the present through a series of dueling definitions and juxtaposed job titles. Over the centuries women have proved exceedingly creative at working around the restrictions placed upon them. When women were not allowed to preach, they renamed their pronouncements prophecy. When women were cloistered from society, they emerged as teachers. When women were denied access to the pulpit, they testified from the pew.

In a twist of nomenclature, when the prophesying, teaching, or testimony of women was at odds with church prescriptions, those opposed to what the women had to say would accuse them of preaching. Such a charge could then be used to silence their voices even though the women had taken great care to label their discourses according to the acceptable precepts of their day. Thus, not only were women told repeatedly that they could not preach, they were also silenced with the charge of illegitimate preaching. Such semantic maneuvering did little to keep women "silent

---

1. John Wesley to Sally Crosby, March, 18, 1769. Cited in Wesley, *Works of John Wesley*, 12:355.

in the churches" (1 Cor 14:34). Indeed, the subject of silence would never have been mentioned in the First Letter to the Corinthians if the women had not been speaking out.

Next to presiding over the Eucharist, the component of worship most vested with claims to authority is preaching. Historically, the church has understood God's word to be present in the act of preaching through the preacher and in the words preached, thereby investing the person of the preacher with extraordinary significance. An attempt to reconstruct, in broad strokes, how and when women functioned as preachers—whether they called it that or not—in the earliest centuries of the church can provide clues for how certain attitudes toward women have become entrenched in church tradition. Obviously, the roles women constructed for themselves, as well as the parts that were scripted for them by others, continue to inform our opinions about women as preachers in the church today. A closer look at this history can help us understand some of our current practices and some of our ingrained assumptions, but more importantly it can move us all, men and women, toward a more faithful construction of the Christian community in which "there is no longer Jew or Greek, there is no longer slave or free, there is no longer male and female" (Gal 3:28).

Assumptions

The case has been made repeatedly that women occupied Jesus' inner circle, they worked alongside their male counterparts to spread the gospel in the first decades of Christianity, and they died alongside men as early Christian martyrs.[2] The question, therefore, is not whether women participated in church leadership, including preaching, but what brought about their exclusion and why did it happen? Though the leadership of women in the church was never free from contestation, the progression of the church through the first few centuries shows a regression of women from leadership in the life of church. Mapping this reality will help us understand the ramifications of this systematic exclusion for women preachers today.

In order to understand when and how women participated in the proclamation of the word during the first few centuries of the church, it is first necessary to know something about preaching during those years.

---

2. See Schüssler Fiorenza, *In Memory of Her*; Ruether, *Women and Redemption*; Torjesen, *When Women Were Priests*; Malone, *Women and Christianity*; Madigan and Osiek, *Ordained Women in the Early Church*, just to get started.

While the New Testament contains speech fragments that might broadly be defined as sermons, there is no extant sermon recorded in scripture.[3] Even Jesus' Sermon on the Mount is widely acknowledged to be a compilation of sayings, to say nothing of the fact that assigning the designation of "Christian preaching" to the one who inaugurated Christianity creates a different dilemma. The speeches of Paul and some of the other apostles cataloged in the Acts of the Apostles might be claimed as missionary sermons, yet nearly all of them follow a similar formula that indicates more about what an early church sermon should be than the text of a specific sermon. From these sermons we can infer that preaching during the first few decades of the church began with a section from the Hebrew Bible, added the claim that Jesus represents the fulfillment of that promise as verified by the witness of the apostles, and concluded with a call for those listening to repent and believe. This basic outline was repeated in large assemblies (Acts 2:14ff.) and secluded areas (Acts 16:13ff.), to hostile crowds (Acts 7:2ff.) and receptive audiences (Acts 11:19ff.).

Sparse information about preaching in the early decades of Christianity is compounded by the paucity of information about women during this time. We learn about the role of women in the first few centuries of the church primarily from three kinds of sources.[4] The first source, official documents such as council canons and church orders, provides valuable information about women's leadership roles by virtue of describing the church's official position on women and prescribing the roles for women in the church. Examples of such official statements include 1 Timothy 3 and later documents such as the *Apostolic Tradition*[5] and *Didascalia Apostolorum*. These sources should be considered very close to the reality for women during the time period they were composed, or at least close to the church's official policy, even if local practices might have reflected a slightly different reality.

The next source is less reliable as an authentic depiction of women. It includes popular narratives and celebratory accounts of women, both fictitious and historical, and tells us more about the social construction of women. The women in these accounts are presented as heroines of the

---

3. Edwards, "History of Preaching," 185ff.

4. Miller, *Women in Early Christianity*, 2–5.

5. Long attributed to Hippolytus, and dated from the early third century; the source and the date no longer apply to this document, however. It could be a compilation of several documents ranging over decades. See Bradshaw et al., *The Apostolic Tradition*.

faith, heroism often taking the guise of defying the cultural expectations for women in favor of ascetic purity. Often the script reflects popular Hellenistic literature of the time, replete with exotic travel, dangerous barbarians, and daring rescues. At the end of these stories, however, union with one's beloved is replaced by a life of "inspiring virtue."[6] *The Acts of Paul and Thecla* and stories about Maximilla, a leader in the New Prophecy,[7] figure prominently in this category.

The final category, formal theological works, provides descriptions of women that reflect the author's model of ideal womanhood. While generally positive, material in this category can be couched negatively so as to link theological distinctions between sin and salvation with women's bodies. Examples of this source include biographies such as *The Life of Saint Macrina* or *The Life of Melania, the Younger*, both of which provide examples of the "purity" of women who avoid sexual activity.

Within the category of formal writing there are only four texts from these early centuries believed to have been written by women,[8] and only one of them, *The Martyrdom of Perpetua and Felicitia*, relates explicitly to the role of women in ecclesiology. The other three are not overtly ecclesial: *The Martyrdom of St. Cyprian*,[9] written by Eudokia, the wife of a high-ranking court official in the first half of the fifth century; *The Pilgrimage of Egeria*,[10] by a woman who apparently occupied the highest social strata of the late fourth or early fifth century; and *Cento*,[11] written in the middle of the fourth century by Faltonia Proba. The fact that we can name all four of these texts also accentuates the paucity of material available about the early church from the women themselves.

---

6. Clark, "Lady Vanishes," 17.

7. The New Prophecy is more readily recognized by the designation the Montanists, but I have chosen to use the name by which members of the community identified themselves. The title Montanists refers to the name of one of its leaders, Montanus, but since he shared power equally with Priscilla and Maximilla, this title also illustrates the diminution of women. Even those who deemed the movement heretical could not pay tribute to the reality that women shared in the leadership of the community.

8. Such a statement does not preclude the likelihood that women authored texts using male pseudonyms and that some anonymous texts were written by women. Furthermore, women had some influence on the writings of men.

9. Kastner, "Eudokia's 'Martyrdom of Cyprian,'" 135ff.

10. Wilson-Kastner, "Pilgrimage of Egeria," 72ff.

11. Clark and Hatch, *Golden Bough*, 1–9.

The value of these writing samples is, chiefly, to demonstrate the difference between how women write about themselves and how men write about women. This is seen clearly in *The Martyrdom of Perpetua and Felicitia*. Unlike the other three writings, this text, dating from the early third century, describes a specific ecclesial subject. Embedded within the narrative is a first-person account of the events leading up to the martyrdom of Perpetua and those who were martyred with her. The work is an intimate and detailed account of the environment of the early church, specifically from the perspective of a woman. Her refusal to recant the Christian faith demonstrates her rejection of conventional society in order to make Christianity the highest claim on her life. The text vividly portrays how this rejection was not a callous disregard for those around her. In fact, Perpetua writes with great pathos of the pity she felt for her father, who "was the only member of my family who would find no reason for joy in my suffering."[12] The most poignant parts of the narrative, however, deal with Perpetua's love for her child. She writes of the terror she felt for the health and safety of the child and the transformation that occurred in her prison cell once he was brought to her.[13]

Unlike *The Martyrdom of Perpetua and Felicitia*, the author of *The Acts of Thecla* remains unknown.[14] Still, this narrative also portrays a woman of strong character, determined will, and independent spirit and provides another glimpse into the struggle that existed between men and women in the early decades of the church. While the story itself contains some mythical elements, the tensions inherent within it are quite real. Where Perpetua provides the portrait of a woman who disobeys her family by confessing Christianity, *The Acts of Thecla* shows a woman who not only opposes her family by renouncing her engagement but also dupes the Apostle Paul in the process by baptizing herself in the face of imminent death. After Paul refuses no less than three times to baptize her, she challenges the institutionalized mandates about who could perform baptisms as well as who could be baptized by self-administering the sacrament. Such acts of "defiance" by women occur against the backdrop of a movement struggling to define boundaries, establish standards, and assign leadership.

---

12. Rader, "Martyrdom of Perpetua," 22.
13. Ibid., 20.
14. Bremmer, "Magic, Martyrdom and Women's Liberation," 36.

Feminine Registers

Exclusions

Clearly, there was no debate about whether or not to include women in the faith community of the early church. They were "initiated into Christ's holy Church, incorporated into God's mighty acts of salvation, and given new birth through water and the Spirit."[15] The words and deeds of Jesus drew no lines between the sexes, and in nearly every encounter with women in the four Gospels, Jesus violated the customs of his time. Mary sat at his feet along with the men being taught. Jesus not only spoke to the Samaritan woman at the well but also requested water from her. Stories of poor widows are told alongside stories of marginalized shepherds, hemorrhaging women are healed alongside crippled men, female prostitutes are called in for supper alongside male tax collectors. Likewise, Paul is clear in his letter to the Galatians that no one should be excluded on the basis of race, class, or sex (Gal 3:27–28). The waters of baptism cover the heads of all. Such a vision takes its cues from Jesus' teaching on the reign of God, a *basileia*[16] of inclusive wholeness with the poor, the sick, and the sinner at its center, women as well as men.

In the first decades of Christianity, worshipers gathered most often in the homes of church members or in a nearby site spacious enough to accommodate the number of people attending.[17] Whether a man or a woman led a particular gathering, women were included as full participants in the meal and worship. Because worship was more fluid in this period, the Eucharist was often observed as a communal meal. Worship leadership, therefore, included responsibility for both proclamation of the word and celebration of the Eucharist. Several New Testament references to "host" families regularly include both the husband and the wife, indicating that in those homes women likely co-presided over the worship gatherings with their husbands, or even presided alone.[18] Given the variety of sources providing evidence that women owned property, managed their own affairs, and conducted business during the first century, it is logical to expect these

---

15. Baptismal formula from *The United Methodist Book of Worship*, 87.

16. Schüssler Fiorenza, *In Memory of Her*, 118ff.

17. For a detailed explanation of house churches and how women figured into their leadership, see Osiek and MacDonald, *A Woman's Place*.

18. Consider Paul's several references to church leaders who bear feminine names—for example, Chloe and Phoebe—and to the couple Priscilla and Aquila. Since Priscilla is named first in Paul's instructions to Apollos (Acts 18:26), she was likely the more active and capable leader. See Shroyer, "Aquila and Priscilla," 1:176.

women would have retained authority when the Christian community gathered under their patronage.[19] As church roles became more clearly defined over time, women still occupied several offices, including presbyters, deacons, and prophets, while the role of widows and virgins continued to evolve. Even though preaching was not the primary task for these roles, it was not excluded from the list of responsibilities.

With the stratification of church roles, prophecy and prayer emerge early as a way for women to voice creatively their pronouncements. Access to an identifiable leadership position—pulpit or altar—is not necessary for the one who rises to prophesy or pray. Rather, prophetic speech originates from the congregation when someone stands and begins to speak from that place.[20] For prophecy a person might begin speaking even before another has finished, allowing the momentum to build as more people are emboldened to speak out and proclaim God's presence. Each person's speech is a kind of short sermon accessible only to those who are near enough to hear it without assuming that the entire community will be silent and listen to one person at a time. Prayer, like prophecy, is also a group activity with many voices joining together in thanksgiving, petition, lament, etc., as worship participants feel moved by the Holy Spirit. Sometimes these prayers assume the form of glossolalia, or speaking in tongues. Since the meaning of glossolalia is not readily apparent, such speech allows women a sense of agency when they might not otherwise speak aloud their faith claims.[21] As appointed male leaders assume more responsibility for the fixed speech within ecclesial gatherings, prophecy and prayer become some of the only vehicles available to women to make a public faith pronouncement.

These informal proclamations are probably the activities Paul addresses in 1 Corinthians when he offers his catalogue for worship behavior (1 Cor 14:26ff.).[22] Paul gives a detailed outline of a worship service, culminating with the infamous directive in verse 34, "women should be silent in the churches." Given that Paul, only three chapters earlier, had provided detailed instructions for how and when women should speak in church, the prohibition against their speaking is incongruent. Because the nature of prophecy allows the possibility for a few assertive individuals to dominate

---

19. Osiek and MacDonald, *Woman's Place*, 12.

20. Wire, *Corinthian Women Prophets*, 183. For a detailed discussion of Christian prophecy, see Aune, *Prophecy in Early Christianity*.

21. Jensen, *God's Self-Confident Daughters*, 125.

22. Wire, *Corinthian Women Prophets*, 146.

the worship gathering, Paul is more likely offering the church worship guidelines. The women Paul cites could be a dominant group within the church attempting to control the worship service by interjecting their prophetic utterances without allowing other voices to be heard. His directive that only "two or three" should prophesy offers a clue to his restricting agenda without necessarily assuming it is a prohibiting agenda.

Beyond worship etiquette, however, the women referenced in 1 Corinthians could represent the nucleus of those whose theological views differ from Paul's. Clues to the theological disagreements between Paul and the Corinthians emerge through the polemics he uses to address the congregation. The Corinthians seem to be claiming direct access to new life in Christ through the Holy Spirit, manifested within their community by renouncing traditional positions of dominance and submission, particularly as those positions relate to women. For example, consider Paul's reminder about proper authority: "For this reason a woman ought to have a symbol of authority on her head" (1 Cor 11:10).[23] At the beginning of chapter 11, Paul sketches a hierarchy that includes himself just above the Corinthians and just below Christ: "Be imitators of me, as I am of Christ" (11:1). He then goes on to draw the rest of the hierarchy scale in the Corinthian community: "Christ is the head of every man, and the husband is the head of his wife, and God is the head of Christ" (11:3). While Paul is decidedly not discussing family systems in this chapter, but rather liturgical space, his order is clear: God, Christ, Paul, Corinthian men, and finally Corinthian women, with some instructional advice on how women ought to comport themselves appropriately. Nowhere is there a total prohibition against women speaking in the assembly. They must simply display the proper decorum.

For women the nuances of the theological disagreement hold less importance than the social implications of Paul's injunction. The status of women within the Corinthian community had risen along with the changing dynamics of education, family influence, and Roman citizenship in society.[24] No doubt, these changes were reflected in church life as well, where women in the Corinthian community found a way to give voice to these shifting roles by using the language of the church to speak of new life and proclaim the presence of the risen Christ among them. Paul, as a dominant member of the old structure (Roman citizen, Pharisaic education, familial prestige), may have had reasons outside of theological difference to

23. Økland, *Women in Their Place*, 176f.
24. Wire, *Corinthian Women Prophets*, 192.

preserve the traditional gender-constructed systems eschewed during the first few decades of Christianity.

The call for order and discipline in Paul's letter to the Corinthians and in the Pastoral Epistles establishes a protocol for the public speech of women that subordinates them to male control even as Roman society is moving in a different direction. The justification for prophecy, however, comes from the Holy Spirit, so those professing to speak for God are difficult to silence. Limiting the prophet implies limits on God's chosen mode of communication. Rather than insinuate that restrictions could be placed on God's voice, the church instituted guidelines for the manner and location of "proper" prophecy.[25]

Especially binding for women in this exchange was the injunction that they must submit their prophetic insight to their husbands or the elders of the church, who would then determine whether it should be relayed to the congregation. Thus, even when the prophetic experience of a woman might be deemed valuable to the congregation, her right to speak it aloud was not. By the time 2 Timothy was written (130–50 CE), what had originated as a quarrel between competing voices of equal merit had crystallized into an imperative against women's leadership. By the end of the second century, prophecy as a category of church leadership began to fade,[26] and not long after, canonization of the New Testament would work a different kind of excluding effect on women by privileging stories about men and including polemical writings against women, a practice that has reverberated through the centuries and influences opinions today.

Renewed interest in the person of Junia (Rom 16:6) illustrates the complicated process of recognizing women as leaders in the early church. The name Junia appears exactly one time in scripture, but for the last hundred years or so it has not appeared at all, having been replaced by the masculine name Junias. Eldon Jay Epp explains this relatively recent name change by making a careful study of the name itself. He concludes that while Junia was a common Roman name, neither of the masculine forms of the name appears anywhere else in the contemporaneous ancient texts.[27] For most of the church's history, the accent for Junia was placed by scribes

---

25. King, "Prophetic Power and Women's Authority," 26–27.

26. This is roughly the time frame in which the New Prophecy began to experience increasing resistance from the centralized power structure of the church, both for their emphasis on prophecy and for allowing women to have prominent leadership roles.

27. Epp, *Junia*, 62–63.

and the name was understood by scholars and interpreted by theologians as a feminine one. Even though Paul cites a healthy list of women who are faithful to Christianity and who serve as leaders in the early church, identifying a woman apostle provoked scholars to search for alternative possibilities. Junia became Junias, a male name, though a name not used anywhere else in the first century. Epp's research helps demonstrate how our current cultural and personal biases influence how we read a text. Scholars translating the name assumed Junia was a man because they think of apostles as men,[28] even when the assumption ignores strong evidence to the contrary.

Other categories of church leadership underwent similar processes of gender stratification. The office of deacon,[29] the lowest rank of the ordained clergy, contains the names of both men and women in some of the early church rolls, but by the third century the task of the female deacon had become only the service of women to women. When Paul wrote the Letter to the Romans, however, church documents interchangeably used the title deacon with a feminine article or included the title deaconess among the list of deacons.[30] The role of the deacon involved charitable, catechetical, and liturgical responsibilities without status distinctions between men and women. Paul's introduction of Phoebe with the title *diakonos* (Rom 16:1–2), a masculine noun, clearly includes the female Phoebe in the leadership of the church. Furthermore, Paul specifies that Phoebe worked alongside him as a minister and missionary of the gospel, not as the servant or helper later translators made her out to be.[31] Paul's reference to Phoebe shows how the plural *diakonoi* included both men and women prior to the third century.[32] Within its time frame, this designation implies that Phoebe is a minister of the church with liturgical responsibilities, which certainly would have included preaching.

Support for deacons as preachers appears in Acts 6:1ff., which makes a distinction between the service of providing meals at the table and the service of word and prayer. The tasks were divided for the very practical reason that there was too much to do.[33] Separating the worship from the food frees those responsible for word and prayer from the burden of also providing

---

28. Ibid., 67.

29. The title of deacon here should not be conflated with presbyterate or deaconate, titles that become more definitive in subsequent centuries.

30. Madigan and Osiek, *Ordained Women in the Early Church*, 8.

31. Schüssler Fiorenza, *In Memory of Her*, 47.

32. Jensen, *God's Self-Confident Daughters*, 59ff.

33. Madigan and Osiek, *Ordained Women in the Early Church*, 12.

the meals. Since the service of word and prayer also includes preaching, those listed among the deacons would have participated in proclamation. It is also the case that those who served meals—namely Stephen in this narrative—both taught and preached as well (Acts 6:9).

In so far as men and women occupied the category of deacon, one who serves, men and women alike shared the responsibilities assigned to a deacon until at least early in the third century when, according to the *Apostolic Tradition*, women deacons are only responsible for the catechesis of women leading up to baptism. Still, during the baptismal ceremony the women deacons have primary authority. They anoint the catechumens' nude bodies, submerge them in the baptismal waters, and clothe them with the white garments of the newly baptized. Only after the newly baptized women are clothed does the bishop join them and impose the final blessing. Even as the women deacons are marginalized by the church hierarchy, they continue to exercise sacramental authority in the baptismal ritual for the women under their care.

Widows and virgins round out the final category of ministerial roles for women in the early church with ramifications for the modern church. Though it was not the responsibility of widows and virgins to preach, the place scripted for these women by the church endures in the attitudes toward women who do preach, especially related to expectations of purity.[34] In order to describe purity we must first understand the words used to describe it—*continence*, *chastity*, and *celibacy*—within their historical context.[35] In common use today, the three terms are basically interchangeable and generally mean abstinence from sexual activity, particularly genital sex. In the time period we are examining, however, these three words carried three distinct expectations. Celibacy defined the state of being unmarried, the presumption being, especially for women, that one does not engage in sexual activity outside of marriage.[36] Continence described abstinence from sexual activity by married couples since those who are celibate are by definition already continent. Finally, chastity meant moral sexual practice within one's state. So, a married person who engages in sexual activity with one's spouse is "chaste," but certainly not "continent." For one who

---

34. Berger, *Women's Ways of Worship*, 90.
35. Macy, *Hidden History of Women's Ordination*, viii.
36. Even here we must bear in mind that a twenty-first-century definition of marriage does not apply. For example, the modern notion of "premarital sex" would be incomprehensible for a woman in the first century. Sex was, by definition, a marital act.

Feminine Registers

is single—celibate—chastity assumes continence. In so far as this relates to widows and virgins, chastity would imply continence because they are not in a state of marriage, but the designation of sexual purity as it is later associated with virgins is not yet the most salient feature.

Like the other categories of leadership in the church, the role of widows and virgins should be understood as a process. For instance, the original designation of ecclesial widows also included the virgins and merely described women who were not married.[37] Widows were those who chose not to remarry after the death of their husbands, as was expected, and virgins were those who never entered into marriage in the first place. Choosing not to marry in either case had less to do with sexual abstinence and more to do with freedom for women from the strictures of a society that expected them to perform as wives and mothers. The choice not to marry carried with it certain claims of agency on the part of women not available to them when they were defined only as daughters or wives. Needless to say, such willful independence could create the kind of havoc in families alluded to in Jesus' warning that "one's foes will be members of one's own household" (Matt 10:36) and in the scenes described in *The Martyrdom of Perpetua and Felicitia*. Fathers expected their daughters to marry in ways that were politically and economically advantageous for them. Refusal to do so could jeopardize more than the chance to bounce grandchildren on one's knee.

As the number of women voluntarily choosing not to marry at all continued to increase, the church found it helpful to create a separate category for virgins, but the emphasis for ecclesiastical virgins continued to be on their decision to forego the status of wife and mother and not on qualifying as one with an "unspoiled" body. While sexual purity is valued, it does not become the defining feature of virgins until several centuries later, inscribing new meanings on a category that originally had different connotations. Through the retelling of stories about women from the past, their lives began to be recast with different meanings. For example, the narratives of Perpetua and Thecla were first told to demonstrate the independence of women from traditional strictures of class and family, but through later church teaching became the moral ideals fulfilling the trope of chastity as purity. When this happens, chastity becomes a category that marginalizes women designated as widows and virgins by segregating them from the public aspects of the church in order to "keep them pure." Purity

---

37. Jensen, *God's Self-Confident Daughters*, 6.

and chastity become descriptors of female sacredness, and impurity and sexuality become descriptors of the profane.[38] Eventually only one avenue leading to holiness remained open to women, "eternal" sexual purity, and other women were pushed toward the profane.

Before this occurs, however, the original stories about Perpetua, Felicitia, and Thecla (and likely other stories now lost to us) offer examples of the struggle over authority for women in the early church, a struggle suggesting women had prominent roles in the life of the church during its first few decades. Other sources provide additional supporting evidence. Paul identifies women as church leaders in the New Testament scriptures, patristic writers praise the witness of women during times of persecution, and the names of women appear on artifacts and tombs from the early church period. Likewise, the Gospel writers did not completely omit the stories about Jesus that involved women, lending further credence to their importance during the earliest stages of Christianity.

Most information about women in the church comes to us through the lens of male writers, some contributing support and others scorn for the women about whom they are writing. While ideas about women written from a male perspective do not necessarily tell us what was going on in the lives of women, much can be surmised from them about ecclesial practices and the biblical witness. By listening to what was being said about women we can infer a great deal of what was going on in the background. Other impressions can be presumed by what was left out. The importance of paying attention to what is not said becomes clear when we recognize how little information about women from the first few centuries of the church comes directly from women.

Because of the paucity of written sources from the first few centuries of Christianity, those at our disposal must be reread with an eye toward those who are silent. Given this reality, inferential information may legitimately be employed to state the obvious truth that women were historical agents during the early centuries of the church's development and that their presence in this development helped shape the life of the church.[39] Scholars readily acknowledge that history was written and compiled by the educated elite of society, namely privileged males.[40] In the process, other voices representing a more egalitarian cross-section of early Christians,

---

38. Macy, *Hidden History of Women's Ordination*, 115.
39. Schüssler Fiorenza, *In Memory of Her*, xvi.
40. Dewey, "From Oral Stories to Written Text," 20.

particularly women, were condensed, marginalized, or suppressed. None of this is surprising to students of historical criticism. Historians generally admit that the writings of the past are less an objective report about events and more an interpretive lens through which the dominant forces of culture offer their perspective. We should not be shocked to hear our knowledge of history has descended through a limited perspective; what we should also be prepared to acknowledge is that our knowledge developed from a perspective that inevitably produced a particular kind of institution, one that systematically excluded the voices and witnesses of women as leaders.

Restrictions

It would be a mistake to compare the preaching of the early church to the sermons delivered in our churches today by credentialed and ordained clergy in a formal liturgical setting. In so far as preaching in the first decades of the Christian movement resembled the exhortation of one who believed in the fulfillment of God's promise through the person of Jesus and who called others to accept this truth, both women and men proclaimed the word whenever presented with the opportunity (Rom 16:3–16). Certainly, there were occasions of "liturgical" preaching from the earliest days of Christianity (Acts 2:46), and in so far as these likely occurred in homes and included a (eucharistic) meal, women would have participated as servers and hosts (Rom 16:3–5), sharing the word and the table. As far as preaching was understood within the church during the first few decades, it appears that women participated in this role. As preaching became more circumscribed by place and time, preachers began to be identified by roles and titles. Gradually these roles and titles excluded women. Women continued to find niches for proclamation, however, even while the official channels narrowed through the centuries. Church documents and letters from church officials from the fifth and early sixth centuries censured those who allowed women to serve at the altar, a censure that would have been unnecessary unless there were some women practicing it.[41]

There is little question that through the canonization of scripture a selection process occurred within the biblical tradition that was not objective or impartial about the role of women in the church.[42] A trajectory of escalating resistance to the witness of women can be traced from the early

41. Macy, *Hidden History of Women's Ordination*, 14f.
42. Schüssler Fiorenza, *In Memory of Her*, 48ff.

writings of the New Testament to the later writings. For example, in spite of the undeniable presence of women among Jesus' inner circle, fixation on "the Twelve" eventually led to the elimination of women as primary recipients of the gospel message. Further, by drawing heavily on Paul's instructions to the church at Corinth, by the end of the second century women were instructed to recount their prophetic experiences to men, who would relay them to the church if the experiences were deemed authentic. Later, an emphasis on purity as a condition for church leadership compounded sexual issues for women in ways that were not germane for men. Eventually, conflicts related to apostolic character and spiritual gifts focused on the sexual status of women. Through silencing and reinterpretation, the role of women was scripted along certain lines and, over time, these prescriptions became accepted without question.

The process of reinterpretation can be demonstrated through the role of widows and virgins. As mentioned earlier, widows and virgins originally were those who had renounced the social status of wife and mother in order to claim the freedom proclaimed by the gospel. Both groups were expected to practice continence, but over time, because virgins had the added distinction of having never engaged in sexual activity, sexual purity became their salient feature. In the process, virgins paradoxically suffered an erosion of their independence in order to protect their sexual purity. The church took their claims of purity to such extremes during one time period that purity had to be "validated" by a pelvic exam.[43] Even though the orders of widows and virgins is not typically associated with preaching, the *Didascalia Apostolorum*, dating from the third century, hints at a power struggle between widows and bishops resulting in the exclusion of widows from all leadership roles in the church, including the role of public speech. Such exclusion would be unnecessary unless they had been previously included.

A similar power struggle occurs with the work of women deacons. While the job description for widows and virgins primarily involved ministering to the sick and poor within the community, with only occasional liturgical responsibility, the role of an ordained deacon included regular participation in worship. Because the lines between liturgical and sacramental leadership are less clearly defined in the first few centuries of the church, absence at the altar does not imply the absence of a role in the liturgy. During initiation rites female deacons were indispensable since the

---

43. Jensen, *God's Self-Confident Daughters*, 21.

Feminine Registers

catechumens entered the font unclothed,[44] and these same deacons also participated in some of the most important parts of the baptismal liturgy. Yet, by the fourth century, when the *Apostolic Constitution* was compiled, a clearly defined hierarchal order was in place that listed bishops in the top tier of ordination and deacons, both male and female, on the bottom. Though deacons did retain the privilege of ordination, such ordination now specifically did not include the role of preaching for men or women. Thus, rather than protecting the authority of women, ordination to deacon meant official denial of the right of proclamation. In this way, the church marginalized women even while continuing to list them among the ordained. By the fifth century, the institutional church had opposed every dominant stream of Christianity that supported the authority of women or allowed for leadership by women.[45]

Things were not so neatly demarcated in the second century, however. The Gospel of Mary offers one example of the variety of theological interpretations present in the church before canon and creed solidified teaching and defined orthodoxy. Since the Gospel of Mary probably circulated in churches during the same time period—early second century—as the Gospel of John, the two of them provide an interesting comparison for how different strands of Jesus' teachings were privileged within specific communities. While the Gospel of John has "always" been heard in the church, the Gospel of Mary remained hidden for over fifteen hundred years. After falling out of circulation during the fifth century, it reappeared in the late nineteenth century when a fifth-century manuscript fragment was discovered.[46] Subsequently, two other fragments of the text were found, although no complete copy of the Gospel of Mary is known to exist. The existing fragments represent only eight pages, probably about one half of the original text. What we have now begins in the middle of a conversation between Jesus and the disciples on the nature of sin. In the remaining pages, we recognize important strands of the Jesus tradition, but a different interpretation of those teachings comes to the fore. Instead of highlighting the suffering and death of Jesus,[47] the Gospel of Mary privileges spiritual

---

44. Ibid., 69.

45. King, "Prophetic Power and Women's Authority" 29.

46. King, *Gospel of Mary*, 3.

47. In fact, the Gospel of Mark is sometimes referred to as a passion narrative with a long introduction, indicating the church's predilection to focus on the suffering and death of Christ at the expense of the life and teaching of Jesus. We would do well to

knowledge as the means to salvation. Furthermore, the Gospel of Mary offers a persuasive statement for the legitimacy of women's leadership in the church, an argument that would not have been put forth unless the church was moving in a different direction.

The main characters in the Gospel of Mary are familiar: Mary of Magdala, Peter, Andrew, and Levi; thus, Mary is obviously drawn from the same oral traditions as the canonical Gospels. Rather than reflecting the Jewish worldview that informed the canonical gospels, Mary draws on the Greek philosophies of Stoicism and Platonism.[48] Mary is not, however, a highly developed philosophical rendition of these schools of thought. It is more like the vernacular version of a sophisticated system. This emphasis on Greek philosophy makes sense if the tradition originated within a Gentile community rather than a Jewish village. The Platonic cosmology and Stoic ethics permeating Mary lend credence to the theory that various communities applied the teachings of Jesus in ways that best reflected their preconceived notions about the world. Even the four canonical Gospels display enough variety to support this theory.

In a particularly telling scene from the Gospel of Mary, Mary of Magdala demonstrates courage and provides comfort to the other disciples. Obviously, the male disciples and Mary had heard the same instruction from Jesus to go forth and preach the gospel, but the eleven remaining male disciples responded by hiding. Because of her calm demeanor and soothing presence, Peter asks Mary to share with them her insight about Jesus' teaching. She does this by recounting a vision, but when she finishes her talk Peter and Andrew criticize her presumptuousness. Levi then reminds them that Peter had issued the invitation to Mary in the first place and opines that their criticism stems from the realization that not only did Jesus share his teachings more openly with Mary, but Mary also understands more accurately what Jesus had to say. Following his harangue, Levi departs with Mary "to announce the good news" (Mary 10:14).

More important than the theology espoused in Mary is the polemic it exposes toward those who would silence women. Since polemics only arise when there is something to quarrel about (note the numerous polemical statements from Paul's letters), it can be assumed that the role of women in the church was contested. The Gospel of Mary supports the leadership

---

recognize that the life and teaching of Jesus incited the suffering and death. Well-mannered carpenters rarely get crucified . . .

48. King, *Gospel of Mary*, 97.

Feminine Registers

of women by reminding the church that Jesus himself warned them about "not laying down any other rule of law that differs from what the Savior said" (Mary 10:13). Even if Jesus never rendered an opinion on the matter of women's leadership, he indirectly supported their leadership by readily welcoming them into his circle. The opposition to women expressed by Andrew, and more vehemently by Peter, in the Gospel of Mary likely represents the voices trying to marginalize women. The reminder that no "new" rules ought to be constructed beyond those dictated by Jesus, coupled with Levi's defense of Mary's superior understanding of Jesus' teaching, hints at the struggle over authority in the church during the early second century. It should come as no surprise that the latest manuscript of the Gospel of Mary dates from the fifth century, a time when the church was becoming increasingly institutionalized and establishing defined hierarchies. Quite simply, Mary "disappeared" because no one was authorized to copy it and the communities for whom the text operated as authoritative had long since been subsumed by the state religion.[49]

The conflict between Mary of Magdala and Peter has deep roots in the tradition connected to disputes over the authority of women. A gospel narrative that privileges one personality will often diminish the other. In contradistinction to the Gospel of Mary, the Gospel of John privileges Peter by framing the events related to Mary in a diminutive manner, even while it is the only Gospel that recognizes Mary as the "first" Christian preacher. For instance, John does report that Mary of Magdala was the first to encounter the risen Christ and the first to announce this truth to the disciples—a part of the tradition so widely accepted that apparently the author could not displace it, though the synoptic writers and Paul managed to ignore it. Still John weakens the role of Mary in these events by having Jesus instruct her not to touch him. No such injunction is issued to Thomas who, a mere ten verses later, is encouraged to "put your finger here and see my hands. Reach out your hand and put it in my side" (John 20:27). Not only is Mary forbidden to touch Jesus, but the Johannine tradition also reports that Mary failed to recognize Jesus when she did encounter him. The character of Mary portrayed in the Gospel of Mary would never have behaved so ineffectually. Meanwhile, John privileges Peter as the first one to enter the empty tomb even though he failed to grasp its significance (John 20:6–9). The Synoptic Gospels go even further, reducing the women's proclamation into a generic

---

49. Ibid., 3.

secondhand report that no one believed and leaving it for the male disciples to verify and affirm the truth of the resurrection.

Read on its own merits as a second-century document circulating in concert with other teachings in the church, the Gospel of Mary frames the conflict between Peter and Mary in terms of preaching and apostolic character.[50] Mary offers an alternative understanding of apostolic succession from the one that was eventually accepted by the church. Mary suggests that simply having heard Jesus is not proof enough that one has correctly understood his teaching and should automatically be granted authority. All the major threads of the Christian tradition support the fact that both Mary of Magdala and Peter knew the historical Jesus, received instruction from the Savior, and witnessed the resurrection. In the Gospel of Mary, however, Mary of Magdala is set apart from Peter because of her exemplary discipleship and keen understanding. Authority to preach, under this rubric, derives from one's spiritual maturity and prophetic inspiration and not on the basis of proper succession. As the church moved increasingly toward a hierarchical structure, solidified eventually by the doctrine of apostolic succession, the Gospel of Mary suggested another method for determining legitimacy.

Another example of the eroding influence of women is demonstrated through the writings of the historian Eusebius. Early in the fourth century he offered a written record of the church from the time of the apostles up to the time of Constantine's victory in 323. Eusebius includes the names of more women than do the next three chroniclers—Socrates, Sozomen, and Theodoret.[51] Furthermore, the three subsequent chroniclers seldom use the names of the women they do mention. The reduction can be accounted for partially by the fact that many of the women about whom Eusebius wrote were martyrs, and after Constantine's edict of tolerance (313 CE), martyrdom did not define Christian witness as prominently as it had before. Even without the gravity of martyrdom to report, however, the failure to mention women implies that significant aspects of church life were devoid of women. Simply put, women were not mentioned by these writers because women did not hold many of the leading roles they had held during an earlier era. As the offices of ministry within the church became increasingly specialized, a place of limited influence was created for women. Women continued to receive ordinations to a number of offices as late as the twelfth

50. Ibid., 176ff.
51. Jensen, *God's Self-Confident Daughters*, 30.

Feminine Registers

century, but as the power of the priesthood increased during the first millennium of the church,[52] the roles for women moved to the margins. The authority to preach, hear confessions, and even participate in baptism, each of which had been exercised by abbesses or deaconesses in earlier centuries, were by the twelfth century reserved only for the priest, an office to which women no longer had access.[53] The well-regarded role of deaconess gradually became little more than "honorary helpers in works of compassion."[54] The designation of prophetess had disappeared by the end of the fifth century, and virgins were sacrosanct.

By the fifth century, as ministerial importance began to be measured by its relationship to the Eucharist, women were on the other side of the altar from those with access to sacramental ministry. This directly affected their access to the pulpit and their preaching role within the church. While the more visible role of preaching the Word and presiding at Table increased, the significance of the supporting roles typically occupied by women decreased. Thus, if Eusebius' successors did not write about women, it was probably because there were none to write about, at least none who mattered in terms of what then mattered for the church and the men writing about it.

While Eusebius does include more women than his successors in his account of the early church, even he is conspicuously silent on the subject of female apostles.[55] The "leading" women described by Eusebius fill roles in a traditional gender script. For example, in his portrayal of Mary the mother of Jesus, her most notable attribute is the virgin birth. Prisca, previously acclaimed by Paul as a leader of the church in Rome, is mentioned only to highlight her perseverance under persecution. The daughters of Philip are described as prophets by an earlier generation, but rather than lauding their zeal for spreading the gospel, Eusebius promotes them as harbingers of virginity. Other women, who were recognized in earlier generations as apostles of Jesus and leaders in the church, are conspicuously absent from

---

52. Macy, *Hidden History of Women's Ordination*, 4ff. Macy is clear in his introduction that comparing the ordination of women in the contemporary church with the ordinations of women reported in the past is a theological matter. As a historian he is specifically interested in "the historical question . . . whether they were considered ordained by their contemporaries according to the definitions of ordination used at that time" (4)—a crucial distinction.

53. Ibid., 41.

54. Jensen, *God's Self-Confident Daughters*, 69.

55. Ibid., 17.

Eusebius' report. Mary the wife of Clopas makes an appearance, but not Mary of Magdala, Salome, Mary and Martha of Bethany, or Junia. Reading only Eusebius, one gets the impression that the spread of Christianity depended solely upon men. This trend of ignoring the contributions of women continues until it reaches the point that women are mentioned only to report on their susceptibility to "heretical" teachings, which led in turn to strict regulations on when and where women could speak or teach. Finally, individual women are no longer singled out for ostracism; instead, the category of woman is deemed suspect. Needless to say, the same categorical generalizations do not apply to men in spite of the fact that quite a few males "distinguished" themselves as leaders of sects later deemed unorthodox by church councils.

Omissions

In his work *Ecclesial Reflection: An Anatomy of Theological Method*, Edward Farley examines the matrices by which canon and creed achieve legitimating status within the ecclesial tradition.[56] He traces the development of authority through scripture, dogma, and institutional structures. Particularly useful for the discussion of the authority of women is Farley's development of the middle axioms. According to Farley, communities identify middle axioms to serve as a bridge between the original revelatory event and the community's application of that event for their life together. Hence, middle axioms mediate divine revelation to the community. They are the conduits of the faith that transmit the content of the faith. As such, they achieve the status of divine authority. The necessity of preserving divine immutability forces the conclusion that what is communicated by means of the middle axiom is "valid and true for all time."[57]

Naturally, scripture, now canonized, occupies a privileged place within the middle axiom, "protected" by the doctrine of inerrancy. Furthermore, dogma—the guidelines for interpretation—and institution—the place of interpretation—join the scriptural canon as middle axioms.[58] Truth, authority, and immutability are used to describe the agents that fill the gap between divine intention and human interpretation. While the process of defining the middle axioms occurs over a continuum, Farley points out that

56. Farley, *Ecclesial Reflection*, 40ff.
57. Ibid., 45.
58. Ibid., 85ff.

Feminine Registers

most of what the church now accepts as "truth" was solidified in the fifth century through the axioms of canon and creed. Once the canon is fixed, the writings inside are binding for the church and those outside lose their influence. After the creeds are adopted, heterodox and orthodox distinctions are clearly recognized.

Shortcomings with the process emerge at several stages along the way. Who makes the decision for canon inclusion will influence which books are selected. Which books are included will influence how divine revelation is interpreted. How divine revelation is interpreted will influence what is true. What is true will influence who has authority. Those with authority will decide the canon and creed, and now we are back to "who," but the status of authority has been rendered moot by the other questions. The canon is fixed, the creeds are composed, and the tradition is transmitted by those with "authority."

God's revelation is now "housed" in selected scriptures (Why John and not Mary?), sanctioned historical figures (Why Hippolytus and not Maximilla?), and authorized institutions (Why Rome and not Phrygia?). The exclusion of women from these middle axioms insures the loss of their voice in the formation of tradition. If there were no women being heard as the middle axioms became solidified into church doctrine, then nothing related to the world of women will be necessary for the church. Worse than being unnecessary, however, is being rendered dangerous. Over time, because of the paucity of women's voices in the places of power and decision within the church, women began to be viewed as obstructions to those who might come under their misleading influences. Women are only included in the life of the church on the condition of their sexual purity, and even then they are treated with a great deal of suspicion because of their ability to "seduce and tempt" the men they encounter. Women who attempt to teach and preach are readily condemned as heretics, not because of what they say, but because of their sex.

One result of such systematic exclusion is that when women do speak or write, they preface their comments with disclaimers like the following, from a letter written in the twelfth century by Hildegard of Bingen: "I am but a poor creature and a fragile vessel..."[59] Women discover that without first humbling their own sex, they cannot presume to offer a valid witness to the faith. Even if there are multiple levels of meaning present in Hildegard's personal disclaimer, the reality is that Hildegard might never have

---

59. Bowie and Davies, *Hildegard of Bingen*, 130ff.

been heard if she had not first acknowledged her subjugated position in society and in creation. She was wise enough to know this and clever enough to offer the necessary self-deprecating preface. Furthermore, Hildegard's description of herself reflects her own experience as a woman marginalized by the church and society even while the witness of her life bore out a resistance to this narrative. Even if later scholars recognize that Hildegard to some degree refused to be confined by cultural norms, the fact remains that she experienced them.

People become what they are expected to be, or, as Louis Althusser suggests, they are "interpellated." In Althusser's words, "ideology 'acts' or 'functions' in such a way that it 'recruits' subjects among the individuals (it recruits them all), or 'transforms' the individuals into subjects (it transforms them all) by that very precise operation . . . called interpellation."[60] For Althusser, the ideology and its interpellative progeny are one and the same. In other words, ideas are institutionalized in practices. As the idea about the role of women became more institutionalized in the hierarchical structure of the church, women found fewer avenues to behave outside of those expected roles. They became what the church told them they were, unworthy and weak or dangerous and deceptive, even while the experiences of their own lives continued to bear witness to a different reality.

Related to this, the scripting of men and women into specific roles within the church creates categories that cannot be easily deconstructed. For instance, when women assume permanent roles within the environs of the church today, they often do so under the guise of cultural feminine norms such as "nurturing" and "mothering." Numerous scholars can now be cited on the matter of gender constructions,[61] and a quick survey of a typical congregation shows women ably filling the roles constructed for them. With rare exception, the senior minister is male and charged with the responsibility for handling the life crises of hospital calls and bereavement situations, while women fill the traditional nurturing role of associate minister, usually the staff person who visits prospective new members and maintains ordinary pastoral contact with the church's constituency.[62] Women also fill the positions of education coordinator, activity facilitators, and day care and after-school directors. Reflecting trends in the wider society,

---

60. Althusser, "Ideology and Ideological State Apparatuses," 48.

61. See especially Butler, *Gender Trouble*. More recently, Fausto-Sterling, *Sexing the Body*.

62. Lehman, "Women's Path into Ministry," 14–21.

women hold the support staff positions of business administrator and administrative assistant. Among the laity, women have historically been the workers in local congregations while men have been the managers. Men serve on the finance committee and board of directors, women keep the nursery and organize the church suppers. While these fixed categories have begun to relax over the last few decades, the repercussions for such "scripting" within the church continue to shape the expectations of the church members who participate in this narrative. For example, a woman may chair the church council, but it is unlikely that a man will supervise the nursery, even if he does spend a few Sundays a year helping watch over it. Thus, when a woman comes forth to preach, the congregation expects her to compose a sermon that highlights cooperation, cheerfulness, and encouragement. Not only should her demeanor reinforce cultural stereotypes, but the content of her message should also reflect their expectations of her personhood.

These expectations have evolved in the church through centuries of systematizing and characterizing women's roles. By the fifth century, women were missing from most of the identifiable places of leadership in the institutional church. Even women who enjoyed a certain amount of agency and privilege within the wider society found themselves expelled from places of leadership and authority within the church.[63] When Constantine made Christianity a state religion in the fourth century, the gradual exclusion of women that had begun at the end of the second century was institutionalized. In this move toward greater stratification, the church also made a clear distinction between who could preach and who could not. As a result the perspective of women is absent from the tapestry of biblical interpretation and church teaching except in unusual circumstances. Moreover, women were not present in the decision-making places and thus could not protest an interpretation that contributed to their own vilification. Obviously, over the next millennium and a half, some women did distinguish themselves by founding and leading monasteries, writing theological expositions, and actively pursuing ministries of compassion and healing. They did not, however, preach, at least in the conventional sense of "the delivering of a religious discourse—a sermon—by a preacher to an audience."[64] When they did, as evidenced by John Wesley's directive to Sarah Crosby, they did not "call it that."

---

63. Schüssler Fiorenza, *In Memory of Her*, 309–15.
64. Kienzle and Walker, *Women Preachers and Prophets*, xiv.

2

Women Now—The Current Situation

The roles women played in the church during the first several centuries are explained through a handful of primary sources, by inference from other prominent sources, and with referral to some secondary sources. The same is not true for the most recent centuries. In these years we have ample evidence of the work of women within the church. In part, this comes from the simple fact that more information exists about all facets of the church because the events are more recent and there are more documents recording them. John Wesley's quip to Sarah Crosby might have been said to any number of women in the early centuries of the church, but the fact that he wrote it in a letter that still exists provides more accurate information about the restrictions and freedoms for women during this particular time period. More recently, minutes from judicatory meetings, denominational publications, and personal testimony communicate much about the shifting roles for women and their emergence into legitimate leadership roles in the church. While applauding the inclusion of women into church leadership, it is also important to ask how women make a difference for the church and what that difference means for the proclamation of the gospel.

Recent Systems

Nearly half a century has passed since women received judicatory approval from many mainline denominations for ordination,[1] thereby receiving

---

1. Admittedly, this is a checkered claim. The Methodist Church granted full clergy

full clergy rights alongside their male counterparts. In that time seminary enrollment has surged from an occasional female student in the classroom to student bodies evenly composed of men and women. In many mainline seminaries, women now outnumber men in the entering class. Many of these women are ordained to word and sacrament and devote themselves to full-time ministry upon graduation. In spite of this reality, our assumptions about women and our practices toward women have lagged behind the official theological reasoning and denominational policies. As women entered the seminaries and filled the ranks of the clergy, most books about preaching and teachers of preaching failed to offer any substantive adjustments related to the arrival of women into the preaching guild. Other than encouraging local congregations not to discriminate against female clergy, little has been said about their physical presence in a site from which they had been systematically excluded for centuries. And almost nothing has been mentioned about the different perspectives and enriching possibilities women bring to the proclamation of God's word.

Three of the most prominent homiletical theorists from the past thirty years—Fred Craddock, David Buttrick, and Thomas Long—help illustrate the claim. In 1985, Fred Craddock published *Preaching* after having introduced his system of narrative preaching in *As One Without Authority* (1971) and *Overhearing the Gospel* (1978). All three of these books privilege a listener-based emphasis on sermon construction. Craddock's work was quickly joined by David Buttrick's *Homiletic* (1987), in which he developed his theory of the "New Homiletic." According to Buttrick, the time was ripe for a new way of conceiving the preaching endeavor after decades of constructing sermons on the basis of explicating theological convictions. To close out the decade, Tom Long published *The Witness of Preaching* (1989, 2nd ed. 2005), offering to the homiletical guild the reminder that preachers come from the community of faith and proclaim the gospel to that same community. Most mainline seminarians, male and female, were trained to

---

rights to women in 1956. In 1974 eleven women were "irregularly" ordained as priests in the Episcopal Church. Presbyterians reflected the Methodists, granting clergy rights to women in 1956, and Lutherans were closer to the Episcopal Church, ordaining the first women in 1970, though not "irregularly." The Southern Baptist Convention, having nothing proscribed about women's ordination prior to 1982, passed a resolution in that year denying ordination to women even though scores of Baptist women were already so designated. Ordination is not synonymous with preaching; however, the two are often conflated. While the privilege of preaching is readily granted to the ordained, it is offered only to the laity under the category of the unusual and infrequent. In theory, therefore, ordination gives women the "right" to preach.

preach using one or more of these texts, yet not one of them has a section dedicated to women as preachers. All three writers make valuable and innovative contributions to the field of homiletics but fail to note a distinction between the preaching of men and women. Such silence subsumes female preachers under an androcentric category that occludes their contributions to homiletics.

Fred Craddock

The inductive style of preaching promoted by Fred Craddock, over and against previous generations of deductive preaching (e.g., Phillips Brooks, Harry Emerson Fosdick, and Grady Davis), might broadly be considered a feminist approach insofar as it is relational rather than determinative. Craddock's book *Preaching* does offer a great deal of material that could easily be appropriated by women in the sections that address the "Life of Study" and "Interpretation," even though he offers nothing specifically identified as feminist concerns to women as preachers or those who train them. In spite of his lack of attention to feminist biblical interpretation, feminist theology, or any explicit acknowledgment of the differences a woman's voice brings to preaching, Craddock's advocacy for inductive preaching resonates deeply with feminist theory. Regardless of where one stands on the essentialist/constructivist divide, there is little debate that women generally engage the world through a more inductive, relational approach.[2]

While our individual assessment systems, including education, place an emphasis on winning and being the best, Craddock interrupts this mindset by suggesting sermons are not autonomous scripts delivered by the preacher from the authoritative position of the pulpit. The pulpit is not a gulf separating the body of people who receive the sermon from the generative process of that proclamation; the people help with the composition, whether the preacher is conscious of their input or not. Using an experiential and expressive style, Craddock summons preachers to focus on the lived experiences of real human beings and insists the core of preaching is an ongoing conversation between the listeners and scripture, which draws on the "deep resonances" of both. Deep resonance, for Craddock, is memory in its fullest sense, inclusive of recall, identity, values, relationships, and hope.[3] Effective preaching not only offers an answer but also gives voice to

2. Jordan, "Toward Competence and Connection," 11ff.
3. Craddock, "Preaching: An Appeal to Memory," 60.

the question, calling out for something from the hearers and letting them bring this question to the sermon in a manner not provocative so much as evocative.

Directing the sermon to the particulars of human experience echoes feminist claims that lived experience is a more valid starting place for theological articulation than deductively explicated doctrinal statements. Instead of starting with a doctrine that must be proved, Craddock insists the preacher must assemble the particulars of experience into a narrative order that culminates in a coherent message. The preacher does more than deposit the answer in the hearer's mind, but brings the hearer into participation in the movement and meaning of the sermon. Listeners thus feel their own feelings, draw their own conclusions, and take some responsibility for the message.

Shaping the subject of the sermon around the listener is not a capitulation to "what they want to hear" but is the recognition that the subject matter of the sermon, the biblical text, first came from listeners on the occasion of their hearing it. The people who first heard the gospel story passed it on to others until eventually it reached us. Now we hear it—or "overhear" it, to use Craddock's term—and pass it on to others. When Craddock speaks of overhearing the gospel he says there are two necessary ingredients: distance and participation. First, distance preserves the integrity of the message—it was here before I heard it and it exists apart from me with its own substance and integrity. The message was not improvised or constructed to suit me but has its own life force and will go on whether I hear it or not. Next, participation explains how the listener identifies with the experiences and thoughts presented by the message because of a general similarity of human experiences. The story told in the sermon and the story imagined by the listener will intersect, but they are not exactly the same story. Instead, the narrative ties the listener to the life of a larger community through a message of memory and hope that conveys movement from one place to another by reproducing and re-creating events. Through this kind of experience the listener is enrolled into a larger consciousness.

It is here that Craddock might offer some awareness of the influence of gender on a listener's experience. The gospel story Craddock hopes will "hook" the listener sounds different when it comes from a woman, primarily because she comes bearing and provoking a different set of experiences that provide the parameters for meaning. When Craddock invokes memory, it only becomes richer for all who listen when it includes and validates what women remember. Secondarily, however, the story sounds different coming from a woman because of the unconscious assumptions swirling around gender constructions in our culture and through our ecclesial traditions. The relational component of preaching shifts when the gender of the preacher changes because of preconceived expectations about women. Craddock's system is driven by this concept of the relational, necessitating acknowledgment of the relational differences women bring to the proclamation of the word. Without such an acknowledgment the distinctive contributions of women are subsumed under an androcentric norm.

When Craddock turns to interpretation, the androcentric norming tendencies of the book are brought more fully into focus. He rightly points to the equal importance of interpreting the listeners, including their context, even as one begins the process of interpreting the biblical text, including its context.[4] Here Craddock could go further and address the contextual gender differences of the listeners. His helpful exercise of jotting down reflections to particular concrete human experiences could be strengthened by the simple addition of sexual identification. "What's it like to be fourteen years old?" elicits a different response from a fourteen-year-old boy than it does from a fourteen-year-old girl. Likewise, the question "What's it like to be extremely poor?" means something different for women than it does for men. Poverty for men and women likely includes food insecurity, inadequate health care, and substandard housing, but these matters are compounded for women by exploitation, subjugation, and exclusion.

Craddock provides preachers with numerous homiletical tools and methods that should be used by both men and women. These tools become even more salient when the variable of gender is acknowledged. Craddock rightly claims that "one cannot totally separate what one hears in a sermon from the one who delivers it."[5] Supposing he would agree that men and women are heard differently, we can readily see how this difference enriches the homiletical possibilities.

David Buttrick

David Buttrick's book *Homiletic* represents another major system on which many of our current homiletic practices are based. The book is divided into two major sections, "Moves" and "Structures," which Buttrick tells us might

4. Craddock, *Preaching*, 84ff.
5. Ibid., 168.

be read in either order. "Moves" describe the parts of the sermon, and "Structures" explain how the parts go together. A move, not to be confused with a point, consists of a single idea that is developed in no more than three or four minutes—the average attention span of a normal congregant, according to Buttrick. Each move has a beginning and an end, between which the idea is developed through various strategies of illustration, clarification, or oppositional phrasing. Moves must work together sequentially, leading from one idea to the next, helping the listener connect experientially to each idea. Here Buttrick, like Craddock, is speaking the language of feminist theory, but also like Craddock he does not overtly name the distinctive experiences women as preachers can bring to the imaging of an idea. Of course, Buttrick claims the focus of this book is on designing and writing the sermon, not on the characteristics of preachers, delivery techniques, or worship settings,[6] so clarifying the rhetorical distinctiveness of women is not his primary objective. Still he offers an abundance of material on language systems and meaning-making strategies that can easily be expanded to note the relationship between language and gender.

Buttrick suggests that for the congregation the design of the sermon operates in three moments of consciousness: immediacy, reflection, and praxis.[7] Having earlier dismissed the third-person viewpoint as too detached for mediating God's presence and concerned about the incomprehensibleness of immediate encounters with God, Buttrick is claiming space for the proclamation of the word that allows the hearer to understand God. These three phases represent different levels of consciousness in the process of mediating God's word. Immediacy describes a process in which the words and the story gradually unfold through analogies of experience exerting "intentional power" on the hearer. In other words, we can see ourselves in this situation and, thus, immediately identify with the experiences within the text. The second moment, reflection, uses a structured field of meaning to see a variety of lived experiences. Without this critical distance the experiences of those listening to the sermon collapse undifferentiated into the experiences described by the text. The reflective moment allows us to consider the meaning of a text without the necessity of a direct correlation to the text. Finally, praxis considers the field of meaning in order to interpret a particular situation and determine a course of action. Such interpretation involves far more than finding scripture to support an act, even

6. Buttrick, *Homiletic*, xi.
7. Ibid., 320ff.

if such a "simple" solution is readily available. Praxis requires imagining God's future, a future not bound by the worldly alternatives readily at hand, and responding to the world according to this new perspective. These three moments—an immediate impression, a deeper impression after reflection, and a change of perspective—offer strategies for sermon design while recognizing all three will overlap in varying degrees even while one moment of consciousness may dominate the sermon itself.

Feminist scholars will hear echoes of their own methodological processes in Buttrick's third moment of consciousness, praxis. Living into the imagined possibilities of new perspectives offers women strength to resist hegemonic systems, tools to tear down oppressive structures, and alternative narratives to describe their lives. Each of Buttrick's moments of consciousness, however, will produce different points of awareness depending upon who describes them. Buttrick himself claims that orientation is crucial in preaching,[8] and the orientation of gender is part of that equation. Certainly, women can construct sermons using each of Buttrick's modes—immediacy, reflection, and praxis—but how those particular moments are mediated to the congregation is altered by the gender of the preacher through her physical presence and by her own sense of self. The identification Buttrick calls for transpires differently when a woman delivers the sermon for the simple reason that she comes bearing a different body, and this identification has direct bearing on what the congregation will hear her say.

Even though Buttrick includes women in the examples he uses to illustrate his points, they appear without any overt awareness that changing the pronoun from "he" to "she" will change a host of other variables related to the points he wants to illustrate. For example, the "human coming-to-consciousness"[9] of which he writes will be a different consciousness for men than it is for women. Claiming rightly that language has the power to "constitute the world,"[10] Buttrick's work offers the opportunity to illuminate how this same language-constituted world is named differently by men than it is by women.

When Buttrick discusses "preaching and authority" and "preaching as hermeneutics," the lacuna of distinguishing between men and women becomes more pronounced. Specifically, for Buttrick authority has the dual definition of power and wisdom, held in tension by the "folly of the cross."

8. Ibid., 347.
9. Ibid., 10.
10. Ibid., 11.

Preaching corresponds to the conventional definition of authority—power and wisdom—while seeking to illuminate the "folly of the cross." Buttrick suggests that rather than assume positions of authority related to power and wisdom, preachers would do well to mediate the mystery of Christ crucified to the "being-saved community,"[11] which resonates with the tenets of feminist theory. It is naive, however, to assume the authority of the pulpit carries equal weight for men and women. Even today, two decades after Buttrick wrote his treatise, women continue to struggle against systems that deny them preaching authority or allow it only under circumscribed conditions, complicating Buttrick's straightforward assessment of pulpit authority.

Finally, in his discussion of hermeneutics, Buttrick comes close to the heart of what is missing when we fail to acknowledge the voices of women in preaching. He suggests preaching as hermeneutics addresses not merely "What does it mean?" but also "*How* do they mean?"[12] By struggling with the question of how the words contained in scripture have meaning for us today, Buttrick rightly illuminates the contextual meaning of meanings. The preacher's consciousness, as distinguished from the Christian consciousness, is the repository for this contextual meaning. The door is now opened wide to discuss the contextual, or discursive, realities faced by women and the diversity of meanings possible through them.

Thomas G. Long

In 2005 Thomas Long revised *The Witness of Preaching*, first published in 1989, and issued a second edition. As in the first edition, Long grounds his comments about preaching in Jürgen Moltmann's declaration that all preachers "come from God's people."[13] He then goes on to enumerate, as he had fifteen years earlier, the positive and negative aspects of the three most common definitions of preacher—herald, pastor, storyteller—before directing our attention to the preacher as "witness." Like a witness in a courtroom setting, the preacher has a truth to tell about something that has been experienced or seen. The preacher is not offering a detached report in the sense of reporting news, but is testifying as a participant in the

---

11. Ibid., 249f.
12. Ibid., 263. Buttrick's italics.
13. Long, *Witness of Preaching*, 303.

experience. The preacher tells the congregation what he saw and what he experienced from his perspective.

The discussion on perspectives is a place where the different views offered by women can be introduced. Certainly, the preacher's perspective should include the work of biblical exegesis and a distillation of the biblical text through the tradition of the church, but the ways in which the preacher gives voice to these topics is shaped by her experiences as a woman no less than the experiences of a man shape his interpretative witness. In so far as men and women experience the world around them differently, they also construe and explain the experience of faith differently. The author of the Gospel of Luke knew something about these differences and chose to tell two stories in order to illustrate God's persistence in seeking those who are lost (Luke 15:1–10).[14] A shepherd holds the starring role in the first story (15:3–7), which highlights his diligent search for a lost sheep and his exuberant joy upon its discovery. The sweeper in the second story (15:8–10) is equally overjoyed upon finding her lost coin, but her search takes on a decidedly different flavor from that of the shepherd. She searches within the house by lighting lamps and sweeping the floor to find her lost coin, while the shepherd combs the wilderness around him to find the lost sheep. Both items were lost through no fault of their owners, both items are found because of careful and thorough attention, and both stories end with a celebration. The lost items, however, generate particular emotions for the one who has lost them and require a search process specific to that item. Likewise, the preacher who is witnessing to her faith experiences particular emotions and describes them through a specific process.

When Long discusses the rubrics of developing a sermon he provides two helpful tools: the focus statement and the function statement.[15] The focus statement—what the sermon aims to say—and the function statement—what the sermon aims to do—grow together into the single idea the sermon wants to communicate. Success in fashioning these statements depends on the preacher's understanding of how the congregation will hear and respond to this particular word from God. Here again, response from the congregation also shifts in relation to the gender of the preacher. Where Long suggests the personality of the preacher influences the form

---

14. The next story in this sequence describes the joy of a father upon the return of his wayward son and is commonly grouped with the first two. Unlike the first two stories, however, the story of the Prodigal Son follows a different pattern and illustrates a different experience of faith. See Hultgren, *Parables of Jesus*, 46–91.

15. Long, *Witness of Preaching*, 99ff.

of the sermon alongside text, congregation, and current events, it should also be acknowledged that gender perceptions will influence sermon form. As noted in the discussion about Craddock, a woman using similar words to relay a faith claim will be heard differently by the congregation than her male counterpart. Because sermons, as Long rightly asserts, are embedded in worship that points beyond itself to God, this difference will have a bearing on the meaning of the gospel for those who hear the sermon.

When Long moves to a discussion about turning the basic form of the sermon into a communicable idea or focus, he mentions the necessity of knowing something about the hearers along with the realization this group of hearers will begin the sermon journey from several different places.[16] Again, such realization should include the multifaceted component of gender, whether those listening to the sermon are men or women. Members of the congregation will assume different starting places for the sermon journey based on their acculturated expectations of women and women as preachers. The familiar images preachers use by way of illustration—simile, analogy, or metaphor—all come coded with gendered expectations. A sermon illustration is not a generic item that, when plucked from the shelf and served up to the congregation, will taste the same regardless of the gender of the preacher or the congregant.

Along with those authored by Craddock and Buttrick, Long's books have been the primary texts used for preaching classes in most mainline seminaries. These three are singled out precisely because they are excellent scholars who have written helpful books. Much of what we take for granted in homiletics today derives from their work. Because of this, the lack of attention to gender distinctions contributes to ongoing androcentric assumptions about preaching. Women who would be preachers get no specific encouragement for the particular challenges they will face. Men who would be preachers receive reinforcement for the dominant assumptions that prevail within the churches. More importantly, none of these writers discuss how proclamation is enriched and enlarged by the voices of women.

Plenty of male preachers have been taught exclusively by men, but no female preachers have been taught exclusively by women. In fact, many women have been taught exclusively by men.[17] It requires a certain degree of

---

16. Ibid., 153.

17. Every class I took in seminary, Duke Divinity School Class of 1988, was taught by a man, and more specifically a white man, with the exception of one: I was taught Black Church Studies by a white woman.

imagination, then, to consider alternative ways of constructing our normative systems, especially when the norms are embodied by particular bodies—male bodies. We must be intentional about naming the distinctiveness of women as preachers. More often than not, this discussion has been tied to the issues of power and exclusion that dominated the last chapter. Because exclusion is still a reality for women in many places, advocating for a woman's right to preach should continue. Those of us who have the luxury to consider physiological or psychological differences in women's preaching will still be dogged by lingering issues of exclusion, even while the conversation starts moving toward expanding the definitions and deepening the awareness of God's presence made known to us by hearing the word through the gift of many voices.

In spite of this daunting project, never underestimate the simple authority of a woman in the pulpit, even if that particular woman never mentions anything related to feminist theory. Her presence speaks volumes, beginning with the message to girls and boys, women and men, that it is normal for women to preach. The pulpit, in and of itself, is a place of authority. Of course, all the trappings of ecclesiology and tradition, historically masculine alliances, shore up this authoritative station. Even so, a woman standing in this place assumes all of that authority. Let her come with ordination and academic credentials and her authority may actually gain some momentum.

Re-claiming Voice: Word as Perfectly Open Sign[18]

Rebecca Chopp began writing about the gift of different voices while most preaching students were studying books by Craddock, Buttrick, and Long. Expanding upon their proclivity to recognize reader response as a helpful tool in constructing sermons, Chopp suggests that language itself is not a neutral variable. Our choice of language influences and even directs the responses of those who hear it. The work of Craddock, Buttrick, and Long is not bereft of this acknowledgment. Each moves toward Chopp's call to eschew simple binary operations. Craddock suggests that listeners must find for themselves the places in the narrative that connect to their lives without being told where these connections must occur. Buttrick wants preachers to recognize the moments of consciousness occurring for those who hear sermons and to craft sermons that draw them into a new perspective rather

18. Chopp, *Power to Speak*, 31.

than dictating exactly what that perspective must be. Finally, Long draws on the rich tradition of "bearing witness" to illuminate how the preacher offers the gospel without controlling it. Even while the methodology of Craddock, Buttrick, and Long leaves behind the hierarchy of pulpit over pew, their use of language sometimes betrays a lack of awareness about how word choices can actually reinforce the hierarchical thinking they are trying to avoid. Words create a world, and critiquing our conventional use of language offers a starting place to examine the transformational possibilities for the proclamation of God's word.

To move preaching toward such transformational possibilities, Chopp challenges preachers to recognize the "two-tier" system that dominates our language use. She begins with the simple claim that the language we typically use employs oppositional terms and dualistic categories. Such oppositional terms result in hierarchical thinking since a positive identity can only be established by construing negative identities in comparison with itself. The positive identifiers become the universal and constant categories by which all other related categories are subjectively evaluated. Such oppositional thinking only serves to reinforce dominant categories, even while it seeks legitimization for the identities under discussion. It is, to quote Audre Lorde, using "the master's tools [to] dismantle the master's house."[19] Thus, for example, the positive image of marriage between one man and one woman is achieved through construing negative images for other family configurations, such as single-parent homes, gay and lesbian partnerships, or even singleness. The "nuclear family" is the sacrosanct norm, and other family configurations are measured by how closely they can approximate this ideal. Such thinking encourages those who would advocate for gay and lesbian marriage to point out the similarities between gay/lesbian marriage and heterosexual marriage in an effort to show that a gay/lesbian couple can look "normal" enough to join the family form. Trapped by dualistic thinking, gay and lesbian couples spend their time and energy trying to look like straight couples rather than celebrating their own gifts and living into their own distinctiveness. Furthermore, the onus of translating this "abnormal" marriage configuration to those occupying the "normative" categories falls squarely on the shoulders of the gay/lesbian couples who must "reach across the aisle" and educate those who think they are abnormal. Imagine if heterosexual couples were asked to explain their marriages to gay couples without reverting to norming categories.

19. Lorde, "The Master's Tools."

Reifying one family model, in this case monogamous, heterosexual life partners, not only allows us to gloss over a litany of shortcomings but also forces the other family models into one homogenous category. More productive for all covenant relationships, to say nothing of those who choose or are chosen by singleness, is a discussion about the distinctiveness each family model brings to the holistic picture of God's creation. The goal is not to balance heterosexual covenant partnerships with same-sex covenant partnerships by making them equal. The goal is to embrace a multiplicity of different family configurations, including singleness as a legitimate basic family unit. In so doing, our language about family systems is enhanced by connectional thinking that understands positions of similarity and difference as mutually enriching rather than as a threat to "one of the most fundamental, enduring institutions of our civilization."[20]

In order to avoid simplistic dualisms, Chopp challenges us to understand that our knowledge comes, not from abstract reasoning that represents a universal norm against which other configurations are assessed, but from three primary places: tradition, experience, and participation.[21] Each of these sites provides an opportunity to critique dominant structures and identify distortions within our epistemological constructions. Tradition, as Kathryn Tanner has pointed out, is "semantically thin,"[22] and what passes for tradition has been selected from a wide array of material that could have been passed down. Thus, knowledge that values tradition disproportionately will always favor the experiences of those who hold power and can exploit their own experiences through hierarchical thinking.

Recognizing, as Tanner does, that tradition refers not only to what is transmitted but also how it is transmitted, Chopp insists traditional interpretations cannot be used to dominate other interpretations simply because they represent the majority. The tradition we have inherited is not that pure, but arises in and through a context of experiences. Other experiences that have been muted by the tradition also participate in the configuration of this tradition, and these experiences cannot legitimately be relegated to inferior positions simply because they are not as well known. To approximate

---

20. George W. Bush, State of the Union Address, January 20, 2004. Of course, in the days following this speech, leading anthropologists were quick to point out the numerous contradictions in the president's claim about historical marriage practices. (For the full text, see http://www.washingtonpost.com/wp-srv/politics/transcripts/bushtext_012004.html.)

21. Chopp, "Cultivating Theological Scholarship," 83f.

22. Tanner, "Inventing Catholic Tradition," 303.

some understanding of these differences, Chopp suggests that rather than formulate our definitions of experience through hierarchical thinking, we should work for empathetic thinking. Empathetic thinking allows us to construe imaginatively how another person experiences the world rather than assuming that person's experience is the same as ours—or worse, asserting it should be. Recognizing how others participate in the tradition through their own experiences allows for a more authentic representation of the tradition. To start the conversation from the place of participation, especially when those places represent suffering or oppression, rather than from abstract claims of superiority, allows us to uncover sources of domination masquerading as tradition.

Chopp names three places where the presence of women or simply feminist processes can move us away from hierarchical thinking and enrich our preaching practices.[23] The first principle involves the awareness of difference. Women are different from men—not better, not worse. Different.[24] Women come to the pulpit bringing a different set of experiences than do men and, therefore, will offer a different description of the lives held in common. Naturally, these differences can be expanded through race, age, sexual orientation, class, etc., but gender is one difference that cuts across all these other differences. It can, therefore, serve as a starting place for recognizing difference and lead to an appreciation of the differences in the other facets of our lives. Even when we cannot know firsthand the particular experiences of another, we can accept the truth that our own experiences are not the norming summation of all human experience.

Awareness of difference points to the second principle named by Chopp: recognition. Once we become aware of the possibilities for other ways of knowing, we are better able to recognize the imaginative potential in our midst. Harriett Tubman, when asked how she managed to deliver hundreds of slaves to freedom, replied, "I could have saved thousands—if only I'd been able to convince them they were slaves."[25] Awareness of the current situation is vital for recognizing the possibilities in our midst. As

---

23. Chopp, "Cultivating Theological Scholarship," 89ff.

24. By naming "difference," I do not intend to initiate a debate between constructivism or essentialism (at least not yet), nor do I mean to imply that all women are different from all men but the same as all other women. I mean only that for anyone blithely to claim it makes no difference whether the preacher is a man or a woman is to betray more about one's own lack of self-awareness than about his or her open-mindedness. Or it is a lie.

25. Cited by Morgan, "Goodbye to All That (#2)."

Women Now—The Current Situation

Harriett Tubman knew, freedom takes on a different meaning for the ones who recognize their enslavement. Likewise, new interpretations for our theological doctrines and symbols are possible when we see ourselves in a different relationship to them. New interpretations, in turn, can open up new understandings of God's presence among us.

These new understandings lead to the third principle for Chopp, a vision for justice achieved by cultivating an epistemological ethic. Such an ethic assumes more than simply the opportunity to speak; it also involves having the necessary resources to join the conversation. The speaker must be respected by those who have typically dominated the discourse. Claiming resources can involve redefining what is important for the conversation. For example, Musa Dube points out that when she came armed with her newly minted doctoral degree from a prestigious American university to a conversation with a group of women from her native Botswana, those women quickly supplemented her postcolonial interpretation of Jesus and the Canaanite woman with their own charitable reading.[26] As a postcolonial feminist scholar, Dube had crafted an interpretive lens identified as Rahab's prism through which to read the Bible.[27] Rahab's prism encourages readers to highlight the historical fact of colonization and its effect on the people colonized in order to recognize the imperialist assumptions within a given text. Readers then move outside that text to create space free from the constraint of colonialism. Employing Rahab's prism for her reading of Jesus' encounter with the Canaanite woman in the Gospel according to Matthew, Dube explained the complicity of Jesus and his disciples in the colonization of foreign lands. When she presented this interpretation to the women of the African independent churches (AICs), she found instead these women had claimed for themselves messages of redemption, hope, and healing in their reading of Matt 15:21–18. "They all assumed that Jesus went there to do good," Dube writes.[28]

This is an astonishing approval rating, especially when juxtaposed with Dube's interpretative move in the opposite direction. Her mea culpa was "my academically informed approach, which is both Western and textual-centric."[29] Expecting concurrence for her claim that the text is inherently imperialistic and detrimental to the cultures on which it had been imposed,

---

26. Dube, *Postcolonial Feminist Interpretation*, 187–90.
27. Ibid., 121ff.
28. Ibid., 187.
29. Ibid., 192.

she discovered instead a creative reconstruction through which the world of the Bible was reconfigured to accord more closely with the reality of the AICs women. From the very text Dube classified as imperialistic, the AICs women glean messages of hope and liberation, which are in turn offered to Dube. In this way, the hermeneutical "spiral" comes back around again and Dube, originally the decolonizing interpreter, becomes the liberated recipient of possibilities beyond polarization. Dube's credentials as a biblical scholar trained in the "best" academic tradition were not the only or even the most important ingredient in the particular conversation where she found herself. Equally important was the context of the interlocutors in Botswana who, through their own faith experiences, understood Jesus as one seeking to do good and not bring harm to those he encountered. Expanding the necessary resources for a transformed vision of justice requires us to suspend our notions of expertise. Questions about knowledge become questions of justice forcing the more salient questions: what counts as knowledge and who has access to it?

Rather than defining knowledge as a finite product, Chopp suggests knowledge is best understood as a process. Recognizing there are multiple ways of knowing challenges the notion that knowledge is a product and invites us to enter the knowledge process. Conceiving of knowledge as a process requires us to abandon our quest for clarity and sameness in order to embrace the imaginative possibilities found in diversity. Chopp reminds us that accepting knowledge as process and not product involves more than adding new ingredients—a few women here, a minority there, perhaps a transsexual for the really courageous. It also involves expanding the discourse to include the concrete practices and experiences where people find themselves and the meaning-making tools they employ to explain these locations. We need, to use Chopp's terminology, a "thick description of the present."[30]

When different voices become part of the public discourse, the experiences they describe introduce ideas that have not been part of the previous "human" description. From women these experiences might include relationships between mothers and daughters, friendships between women, and an understanding of God's presence mediated through domestic tasks. Since the incarnate God works through the particular and the concrete, our traditions about God are never more than the codified experiences of particular people who narrated, wrote, and passed down what they knew.

30. Chopp, "Educational Process, Feminist Practice," 115.

All theology is such a rehearsal of using experience to make sense of God's work in the world, but until recently only particular experiences were considered legitimate for theological discourse. Opening the conversation to different voices allows us to employ a different process for describing God, a process that does not replace the more conventional definitions but supplements and enhances them.

Once we admit knowledge is constructed in and through history, not abstracted from it as universal truth, we can understand how knowledge is linked to power. Thus, epistemology is always an ethical process grounded in questions such as the following: Who benefits from this knowledge? Who is harmed by not knowing? What counts as knowledge—abstract factual information or experiential, relational, imaginative possibilities? Knowing God is about more than reciting a formula, like the Nicene Creed, or memorizing a definition, like the Small Catechism, though such formulaic recitations have served as faith-proofs on numerous occasions. Experiencing God's presence through the practices of the community and the formation of one's habits often accurately reflects knowing God. According to Christian teaching, the responsibility to compose one's personal narrative is best done through community, but the dogmas of that community's tradition need not determine who we will be. Rather than conceive of knowledge as objective or autonomous, we should understand knowledge as coming from past traditions, contemporary situations, and future possibilities.

By moving from the particular historical experience to the transcendent possibilities and then back to the particular, a new narrative begins to take shape that calls into question the dominant story. Take, for example, the commonly held notion that girls cannot play baseball. Except for the occasional female prodigy who breaks the gender barrier and plays Little League, a quick look at the major league and farm league teams bears out this truth. Even the girl who plays Little League generally ages out of such "radical" behavior before she is old enough to mount a challenge to the high school varsity team. So it is that the truism, girls cannot play baseball, lives on. There is another story, however, the story of the All-American Girls' Professional Baseball League, which thrived in the United States during the 1940s.[31] While the women may have played the game with as much passion and skill as their male counterparts, femininity was still a high priority for the players: the women played in skirts, they were required to attend "charm school" each evening after practice, and they adhered to

---

31. Lesko, "League History."

a strict code of conduct that included curfews, language censoring, and proper etiquette for every situation. A few years ago Hollywood exhumed the story and made a movie about the league, thus retelling the dominant baseball narrative with a different set of particulars. While the movie did not bring about a sudden influx of women into the baseball farm leagues, at least no one can claim without dispute that girls cannot play baseball. This particular baseball instance changes the universal baseball narrative.

The stories we tell ourselves define our "we."[32] Acknowledging that the "we" fails to represent the whole, it remains the case that our identity is formed by the stories we tell. In order to shape a new identity, we must tell new stories. Telling new stories involves both remembering things that have been forgotten as well as speaking aloud those truths that have been historically silenced. The new stories often meet with resistance from the hegemonic majority, that group which shaped the dominant narrative, but the marginalized minority will also resist the disruption of their narrative, which even though offensive is nevertheless familiar. New voices are essential in order to hear new stories. Chopp suggests that a narrative identity shaped by multiple voices has three fundamental characteristics:[33] the narrative must attempt to tell the truth by pointing to the absolute through the particular; such truth-telling then summons attention to the other; finally, attention to others will lead to a discourse that is more diverse. The aim of such a process is to bring the content of our preaching more in line with the context in which we preach it.

Enriching Inclusion

For much of the church's history in most circumstances, women answered the call to preach by circumventing the channels of authority denied to them. Thus, the news for the church in the twenty-first century is not that women are finally claiming their voice and winning the right to speak out, but rather that women are reclaiming what was normally practiced in the earliest decades of the church and creatively performed in subsequent centuries. The task remains, however, to find this voice in an institution that has lifted the ban on women's speech with the caveat that women will say what they are "supposed" to say and will perform according to conventional gender expectations. Whether they are men or women, both those

32. Chopp, "Reimagining Public Discourse," 36.
33. Ibid., 40ff.

who hear sermons and those who deliver them harbor many of these expectations and conventions. Recognizing the conventions that shape us and acknowledging the expectations we embrace can help initiate new patterns of behavior.

As Chopp has explained, our traditions, experiences, and practices are crucial to our interpretation of the world around us. When different experiences call for different practices, we begin to think differently about the traditions previously taken for granted. The influx of white, middle-class women into the workforce during World War II as "replacements" for the men, and then in subsequent decades as a means of augmenting family income, has made the work of women a recognized topic. Women have always worked, but shifting the locus of this work to the public sphere focused attention on the gendered identification of the work they had always done without pay and without recognition. Other women, of course, have always worked outside the home, either in the homes of privileged women or in low-paying jobs that were not "counted." Even while the labor force now includes women across class lines, it remains the case that women on the whole continue to toil in low-paying, "feminized" jobs.[34] Latent within any discussion about women as preachers are these gendered expectations about work.

Furthermore, the development of reproductive technologies and the marketing of birth control pills in the 1960s provided another cultural shift in the lives of women. Until then, abstinence had provided the only safe method of birth control since, aside from being illegal, abortion often carried greater physical risks than giving birth.[35] Reproductive choices and improved health care have combined to offer women longer lives without lengthy years of mothering work. Work that dominated the adult lives, and sometimes the adolescent lives, of women in the past now lasts only a fourth to a third of a woman's adult years. There is time to do other things. There is space to hear God's call and to bear proclamation of the word.

Related to, but distinct from, reproduction technology, new attitudes about sexuality also open new avenues for women. Even if Christian

---

34. According to the U.S. Department of Labor, 80 percent of women who are employed outside their own home work in jobs that pay the lowest 20 percent in salaries (Bureau of Labor Statistics, *Women in the Labor Force: A Databook* [2007 edition]). A number of scholars have discussed the "feminization of labor"; see in particular Malos, *The Politics of Housework*; Lazzarato, "Immaterial Labor"; Hochschild, *The Managed Heart*; and Salzinger, *Genders in Production*.

35. Degler, *At Odds*, 227–28.

teaching and church polity have done little to acknowledge different understandings of sexuality and changing sexual practices, both realities are redefining the lives of women and men. A glance at the magazine rack while standing in the checkout line of the grocery store or ten minutes in front of the television will confirm the claim that sexuality dominates our culture. Women and men need constructive ways of addressing this dominant motif in our lives beyond falling back on provincial dogmas that have little significance to the lives we are living.

Changes in reproduction and sexuality offer different perceptions of the family. A variety of family patterns have existed throughout history, and the "nuclear" family we hold so sacrosanct is a fairly recent addition to this lineage. Nevertheless, because the nuclear family model has dominated in this country since the early nineteenth century, it provides the litmus test against which all families are measured, even while it no longer represents a majority of family forms.[36] Single-parent families, usually mothers, have risen dramatically over the past four decades. Same-sex couples are openly acknowledging their covenants and opening their lives to the care of children. Never before married, single adults are likewise becoming parents. Other adults are choosing to remain single and childless. Through each of these configurations, different family patterns emerge that allow women to think differently about their own partnership and parenting options.

Finally, the awareness of violence against women and children demands our attention. Whether violence is actually on the rise or whether we have a heightened awareness of what has always existed is not the issue. The Centers for Disease Control and Prevention lists domestic violence against women as a leading health threat for women in the United States,[37] making this a matter of grave concern for all people, not just women. Recently, the church has begun to acknowledge partial complicity in this reality, brought about implicitly by its silence and explicitly through some of its misogynistic teachings.

Each of these factors contributes to shifting dynamics in the lives of women and has helped open new channels for the (re)emergence of

36. Though certainly not statistically reliable, it is the case that at a recent gathering of twelve of my closest friends from college, both men and women, only three of us occupied a place in a "nuclear family," a heterosexual marriage with two or more children. The other nine were atypical, albeit the majority.

37. Approximately 1.5 million U.S. women are raped or physically assaulted by a current or former spouse, cohabitating partner, or date each year. See Tjaden and Thoennes, "Prevalence, Incidence, and Consequences of Violence against Women."

women's voices in the church. Their voices sound across a landscape that no longer takes for granted many of the expectations about sexuality, family configurations, gendered divisions of labor, or "traditional" theology. What we know about any of these categories is malleable for the people living through them. What we know about our lives and the forces orbiting around them is always in process. By adding their voices to these processes and becoming an integral part of the narratives, women provide a critique of the inherent sexism of the Christian tradition, in so far as it values men over women, assumes the masculine experience is also normative for women, has imaged God with predominantly masculine metaphors, and has even used the Christian message to support or defend violence against women.

Substantial evidence has been assembled to demonstrate how religious and theological views about women have contributed to subordinating social structures for women as well as to their own negative self-perceptions. The pervasiveness of androcentric thought through centuries of biblical interpretation and theological construction has, in some ways, distorted the teaching itself. The visible and vocal presence of women makes a difference in the church by enriching the theological and semantic possibilities that circumscribe our traditions, determine our experiences, and dictate our practices. Rather than detract from the proclamation presented by men, women's voices enhance the linguistic possibilities by challenging and rearticulating conventional knowledge within the church. This, in turn, adds depth to what has been routinely accepted without question. New voices bring new perspectives that can enable the church to reinterpret the old, promote the good, and imagine the new, not in ways that devalue inherited knowledge, but in ways that enrich our theological and ecclesiological practices.

Early feminist scholars began this process by challenging some of the accepted "conventional wisdom" about women in scripture and in the church. They discovered women did play vital roles in the interpretation and spread of the gospel but were often written out of the story by later generations of interpreters. Recognizing that interpretive communities often function to promote their own self-interests led scholars to look "behind" the texts and the doctrines in order to illuminate the presence of women in the tradition. Forgotten leaders and overlooked movements were excavated and studied with an ear towards what is not heard. For instance, if we hear scriptural claims that women ought to be silent in church, what are we not hearing about the reasons for such an injunction? Other scholars focused on biblical women, long seen only as appendages to the male heroes of scripture, with an eye towards their particular motivation and agency within the narrative of scripture. Through this process of discovery, expression, and interpretation, all the parties within the conversation are held accountable for the stories we tell, and the stories begin to express deeper significance for the lives we live today.

The fundamental principle that both men and women share fully in human nature and both are valued equally in God's eyes leads to the realization that neither is closer to God or created more perfectly in God's image. Exposing the false dualisms between men and women, spirit and matter, soul and body, etc., invalidates the hierarchical arrangements that mask and muffle the rich diversity women bring to homiletics. It is incumbent upon a feminist homiletic, therefore, not simply to make sense from a feminist perspective, but to provide an alternative understanding of the homiletical enterprise. Raising homiletical questions forces us to deal with ecclesiological matters in so far as one's ecclesiology determines who may preach. Those complicit in the current ecclesiological systems that prohibit or inhibit women's preaching include both men and women, many of whom are unaware of their roles. A crucial first step comes through recognizing how our theological and ecclesiological frameworks influence our preaching practices. While Rosemary Radford Ruether, Elisabeth Schüssler Fiorenza, and others have become household names in seminary hallways, for the most part the framework for preaching remains conventional because much of the theology and many of the educational practices underpinning homiletics are still androcentric. Since understanding God's revelation does not come from preaching the sermon, but by engaging in the theological process, it behooves us to enrich the framework with feminist insights on theology, biblical studies, and liturgy. In this way traditional gender asymmetries are not merely eclipsed but are rendered invalid as a theological foundation.

The voices of women, therefore, are not added to the homiletical soup in order to balance the flavors by equalizing the hierarchies. The voices of women create new soup by transforming the ordered hierarchy of language into a multiplicity of connected differences. The absence of women's voices from centuries of Christendom is not merely tragic for those women whose voices were rendered mute, but is also lamentable for all who did not have the privilege of knowing the distinctiveness they might have conveyed about the presence of God and the richness they might have offered to our current understandings about God. Diagnosing the distinctiveness of women's voices and exploring the richness they convey about the presence of God requires taking a detailed look at the meaning-making strategies used by those who preach and those who listen. It requires understanding the register of a sermon.

3

What, Who, and How
—The Real Meaning

A number of analytical systems might be used to help show the distinctiveness of women's preaching. The concept of register, first developed by M. A. K. Halliday in *Language as a Social Semiotic* (1978) and further refined by John Frow in *Marxism and Literary History* (1986), is one such tool. Halliday defines register as "the configuration of semantic resources the member of a culture typically associates with a situation type. It is the meaning potential . . ."[1] Register offers a process for understanding how meaning extends through and beyond the spoken words. Meaning comes to life by considering not only the words themselves but also the social contexts in which the words are spoken, the relationship between the communicating parties, and the method of the communication. Listeners make choices based on patterns in each situation and then construct the meaning of what they hear. The choices made by listeners will have as much bearing on what is heard, if not more, than the content of the communication itself. Choice, of course, is a debatable term since choice is readily influenced by our multiple discursive positions. Diagnosing the ingredients of our choices and the process of making meaning out of what we hear can help illuminate many of the preconceived notions and norming expectations faced by women preachers. Once we understand how these variables influence our

---

1. Halliday, *Language as Social Semiotic*, 111.

hearing, we can develop new strategies for preaching that enable a fuller representation of women's voices in the proclamation of the gospel.

To explain the operation of register, Halliday identifies three variables that overlap and interlock to produce the meaning made by a particular communication event; they are field, tenor, and mode:

1. Field refers to both the subject matter and the social process in which the subject matter is grounded—what and where?
2. Tenor defines the role relationships among the participants—who?
3. Mode describes the form of the semiotic medium—how?[2]

Field, tenor, and mode are not components of speech, but rather determinants, collectively serving to predict the meaning a listener will make of what is heard.[3] At the intersection of these variables the communication comes to life through the constellation of meanings in the particular social system. A conceptual framework governs the production, transmission, and reception of appropriate meanings in appropriate forms in appropriate contexts. In other words, we don't tell jokes at a funeral. These normative systems specify what can properly be said at a given place and time. Parents "coo" at their infant children; drill sergeants do not coo at their recalcitrant soldiers. When they do, everyone present interprets it as sarcasm, not as endearment for the soldier. The correct meaning of the coo is derived from the constellation of all the variables. In order to determine the meaning correctly, what is said cannot be separated from where it is said, who is saying it, and how it is being said.

Like a nursery rhyme or a military order, a sermon has its own particular register that can be analyzed through Halliday's variables. Each variable provides crucial information for the potential meaning of a sermon, meanings that are brought to bear on the sermon by those who hear it. Because the person of the preacher is an integral part of the message, each variable is further influenced by the preacher's gender. Of course, gender most influences the variable defining the relationship between the speakers, but expectations about gender differences also create variable shifts in

---

2. John Frow points out that Halliday is vague on his definition of field, using it to refer "to a specific semantic domain or 'subject matter' and to the ongoing social process in which participants are involved and of which this semantic domain is one manifestation." In other words, field identifies both content and context, what and where. Frow, *Marxism and Literary History*, 68.

3. Ibid.

context and method that can alter the presupposed meaning of the words. Using register to examine the importance of gender for preaching allows us to move beyond merely analyzing sermon content in order to learn something about the entire domain of meaning in the sermon and the distinctiveness that women bring to the preaching event.

Obviously, sermons are closely tied to a particular rhetorical and linguistic form, but register forces us to move beyond the simplistic notion that a particular text or theological concept will always mean the same thing throughout time and across a variety of situations. By helping us recognize the distinctiveness of the different sites where meaning is produced, register provides a diagnostic tool for evaluating the appropriateness of these interpretations. Situating preaching within this kind of discursive process allows us to examine the influence of social locations, gender constructions, language operations, and the instability present within each of them. While gender constructions, social locations, and language operations are deeply entrenched in our culture and our psyche, they are not permanent and unwavering categories. They are, in fact, unstable or only temporarily stable. The stability of their meaning depends on the other signifying processes and social practices that hold them in place. These processes and practices sometimes reproduce the expectations of communicated meanings, but at other times can alter the assumptions to introduce new meanings.

As mentioned above, gender, as it gives definition to who is speaking, has a great deal of influence on what is heard. Thus, changing the gender of the speaker will alter the possibilities for meaning contained in the other variables. Changing one variable creates subtle changes in meaning, but changing a variable as significant as the gender of the speaker introduces the possibility that the entire communication will be altered even when the other two variables remain constant. The potential for different meanings begins with the content choices made by the preacher, and while it is far too simple to claim that women make different choices than men—many times they do not—it is not a stretch to suggest that they might. At a deeper level, however, a woman's presence in the pulpit has already shifted the content by changing the context of who may preach. This change will alter the subject of her sermon before the first word is spoken. While the preacher might intentionally create this register shift, in many cases the meaning changes without the preacher's awareness simply because she shows up, and then changes even more based on the choices made by those who hear her words.

Field: Content—What?

In Halliday's register schema, content and context—what and where—are more complex than they first appear. While the content of the sermon may seem easy to identify, the interpretive strategies employed by those who hear the sermon offer a range of meanings for the subject matter addressed in the sermon. For preachers, of course, the subject matter is God, but more particularly God as revealed through scripture and interpreted by the tradition. In order to make meaning of a particular text the preacher and the congregants bring their interpretive lenses to bear on the biblical text and the proclamation issuing from it. These lenses are shaped by the historical, political, social, and religious horizons they inhabit.[4] In other words, when approaching a given text the preacher's decision about how to construe that scripture passage will guide the choices about how to use the text. Other knowledge sources around the preacher influence the preacher's choice of content for the sermon. For instance, the Bible states the world is flat, but no twenty-first-century preacher would announce that fact because of what we know about the universe. Thus, the Bible is not called upon to answer the question of a flat world and is not deemed right or wrong by virtue of the answer it provides to this question. Instead, what we know about the shape of the earth informs our reading of the Bible on this particular subject. Simply stated, preachers know more than what they read in the Bible, and they compose sermons using more than the text provides. Likewise, the members of the congregation are making their own interpretive decisions about the text and listening to the preacher's interpretation through that lens. This convergence of knowledge provides another interpretive tool for diagnosing the content of a sermon.

Barbara Holdrege, in her article "Beyond the Guild: Liberating Biblical Studies," helps explain the process preachers and congregations go through to decide what scripture is saying. She points out that the text, as the word of God, must always be in relationship to the community of faith.[5] Scripture is sacred and authoritative for the community only in so far as the community finds within it the means for understanding its life. For the community, the historical, literary, and cultural aspects of the text never supplant the power of the text to speak to the community hope in the midst of despair, peace in the midst of strife, or life in the midst of death.

---

4. Kelsey, *Proving Doctrine*, 160ff.
5. Holdrege, "Beyond the Guild," 139.

Feminine Registers

For the faith community, the question is not so much about what and how the text was produced—information sought by the historical, literary, or cultural critic—as what has been produced by the text and is continuing to be produced each time the community engages this text as scripture. This kind of relational understanding of scripture is at the heart of preaching since the task of the preacher is to relate this sometimes alien word of God to the lives of those who hear the sermon.

Relational interpretation does not throw the doors open to relativism. The community that defines itself in relation to the scripture will also define the appropriate rules for interpretation, proclamation, and response. Perhaps preaching, more so than some other disciplines, is better equipped to respond to the charge of relativism because of its relational quality. In his book *Confessing Jesus Christ: Preaching in a Postmodern World*, David Lose maps one strategy for the relational approach to sermon construction:

> The first [stage] deals with *approaching* the text on behalf of the congregation. The second describes our *listening* for the text's distinct confession of faith. The third concerns *discerning* what that confession may mean in light of the rest of the canon, the community's context, and one's hermeneutical experience and expectations. The fourth involves *articulating* that new confession for the community so as to actualize the text and offer it to the community to be appropriated through the power of the Holy Spirit.[6]

Lose explains preaching as a confessional necessity evoked by an encounter with the word of God. Confession, here, is a means of testifying to a particular relationship with the word and is not a way of proving its "ultimate truth."[7] Likewise, "approaching the text on behalf of the congregation" involves understanding a great deal about the congregation.[8] A hermeneutical circle must be at work even as scripture takes the lead position in the hermeneutical dance. Furthermore, the congregation itself has already influenced the approach to scripture being made by the preacher on behalf of that congregation. The confession made through the text on their behalf will bear the marks of their influence.

---

6. Lose, *Confessing Jesus Christ*, 189.

7. Ibid., 138.

8. See Tisdale, *Preaching as Local Theology*, 56–90. Tisdale argues that the preacher needs to spend as much, if not more, time "exegeting" the congregation as she does exegeting the biblical text.

Content is not the last word on the meaning of a sermon even after careful consideration of the scripture. The relationship between the communicating parties at work in the hermeneutical circle has bearing on the content. The mode or method of sermon delivery, as manifest through tone, tempo, and timbre, influences how the content is heard. For example, shouting Psalm 51 would produce a different meaning, probably a dissonant meaning, from the one we typically associate with David's confession. Changing how the psalm is heard might give it a meaning altogether different from the confession we have come to think of those words conveying.

Because the traditions and practices of the community provide the rules for interpretation related to the text, further judgments are needed about the tradition that produced such an interpretation. This judgment, in turn, is based on the traditions and practices from which it emerged. Such reasoning does not make the interpretations relative so much as it makes them relevant, but the possibility remains that they are not relevant for all people at all times. Within a particular setting, certain interpretations will always be "wrong." Such a value statement, however, only holds credibility within this discourse, and the same interpretation in another setting might just as readily be "right." Content alone will seldom provide unanimous and lasting meaning. If it did, women would never preach, Southerners would still own slaves, and same-sex covenants would always be illegal.

In these instances, accountability to the truth must come from another source,[9] allowing the context for receiving the content to help determine the validity of the pronouncement. By introducing alternatives to the dominant perspective, the preacher challenges the congregants to reexamine their views in light of new ideas. Likewise, reservations from the congregation toward the preacher's position challenge the preacher to reexamine her perspective in light of questions raised by the community. Such mutual reexamination facilitated through the relationship of preacher and congregation offers the possibility of refining the message in ways that are, in the long run, more consistent with God's word. Allowing the text to speak anew with each reading will not strip it of concrete substance or reduce it to arbitrary relativism. In fact, several right interpretations might emerge from the same biblical source without the necessary burden of offering a single, determinate truth. Adhering to monochord truths denies

---

9. See Fish, "Is There a Text in This Class?" 314: "The introduction of new categories or the expansion of old ones to include new (and therefore newly seen) data must always come from the outside."

the creative power of God's word and insults the reasoning abilities of the ones to whom God directs this word.

Still, preachers have disproportionate power in the homiletical process in everything from the selection of texts to the plethora of illustrations used to elucidate this text. Even preachers who rigidly follow the lectionary and painstakingly observe the seasons of the Christian year retain a high degree of freedom when it comes to text selection and its exposition. The preacher's favorite commentary, the illustrations that come most readily to mind, and the preachers' interpretive lens influence the content of the proclamation. Suppose, for example, pride is the subject being addressed by the preacher. One might address unbridled pride as a manifestation of sin, the prevalent definition in conventional theology, and then proceed to laud the attributes of submission to God's will and humility before God's grace, both of which are regular and suitable themes for Christian preaching. For someone who is oppressed or abused, however, submission to authority would not be an antidote to sin and might, in fact, lead deeper into sin. The proper response in such a dehumanizing situation would be resistance and refusal, a dissonance that could generate pride rather than diminish it. So it is that those who hear the sermon content make self-determinative judgments about pride's value from their own individual situations.

Obviously, the preacher's illustrative choices, theological tendencies, and personal proclivities will do much to influence which definition reigns in the minds of the congregants. Furthermore, listening to an illustration about pride—content—from a place of oppression—context—can change how we think about both the content and the context. Context as it relates to the field variable in the preaching register can supply a shift in meaning even when the sermon content remains virtually identical.

Field: Context—Where?

The content of the sermon appears self-evident, but precise definitions will shift in relation to the other linguistic variables produced within the register constellation. One of these shifts can occur when considering the context of the interpretive lens. Where the communication occurs, however, involves not only the physical location of the speaker, but more importantly her social position. For the one delivering the sermon, her physical location is simple enough to identify even if all locations are not the same for all preachers. Some preachers remain fixed behind a pulpit, while others roam the chancel area or even the entire sanctuary, but unless the preacher is a guest she will be where the congregation is used to seeing her. The preaching function places her in the correct location for sermon delivery, and even a guest preacher usually tries to behave according to custom by asking a few discrete questions prior to worship. This site, of course, imparts its own systems of meaning through a variety of pretexts that will be discussed more fully in the next chapter.

Grasping the social location of the preacher, however, requires paying attention to the discontinuity between her social position and her discursive position. The negative impact of such discontinuity forces women to rationalize and even apologize for their presence in the pulpit, the discursive position, because of the gendered stereotypes imposed by their social location. From a positive perspective, the confluence of these two sites can interrupt the presuppositions of the sermon register and enable new meanings of the gospel to emerge. Using the tools of feminist theory to analyze the discontinuity between the social position and discursive location of the preacher helps explain how these different meaning-making possibilities emerge.

For the woman who would preach there are social forces embedded in her life affording her a particular "standpoint." From this place she views the meanings in orbit around her even while she participates in the construction and continuation of those meanings. As previously mentioned, the text and tradition contribute a great deal to this assembly. Their intersection with the specific lives of women and the larger social forces in which these lives are embedded provide the standpoint, the context, from which meaning-making begins. Knowing a little about standpoint theory can help explain the connections between the specific lives of women and the larger social forces around them.

Early proponents of standpoint theory focused on a simple analysis of labor.[10] Arguing that the oppression of women is hardwired into the very fabric of creation because only women are capable of bearing children, designers of standpoint theory first diagnosed a universal or original oppression of women. According to them the definition of labor includes not only the production of goods but also the production of the society from which comes the producer of goods. Women birth the babies, who grow up

---

10. For a detailed account of standpoint theory, see Hartsock, "The Feminist Standpoint," and Haraway, "Situated Knowledges."

to become the workers, who are fed and clothed by women, who send them back into the work world. In other words, women reproduce the producers.

According to Kathi Weeks, such a simple labor analysis does not fully expose the pervasiveness of "patriarchy" defined as "a system of hierarchy, privilege, and domination exercised by men over women."[11] In Weeks' definition, women are subservient to men at every level of the class system even if all men do not oppress all women. Hence, an upper-class woman may dominate a working-class man, but he will in turn dominate working-class women. Meanwhile, the upper-class men will dominate the upper-class women. Thus, a collusion of "capitalism and patriarchy" informs the systemic oppression of women, a system that is most clearly illuminated by the gendered division of labor.[12] This system provides normative assumptions about what women should do and what men should do. Assumptions that start off as simple job distinctions—women wash the dishes and men take out the garbage—can easily morph into roles that are restrictive and demeaning for women. These gendered labor divisions affect the context when women preach and are reinforced by negative portraits of women from the text and the tradition.

Weeks diagnoses the gendered division of labor by focusing on three concepts: totality, labor, and standpoint.[13] Totality, according to Weeks, names how we understand the connection between the everyday practices of our lives and the social structures framing our world—to cop a phrase, the personal is political. Secondly, to understand labor, Weeks points out the connection between what we do and who we are. Because gendered divisions of labor determine much of what we do, Weeks believes it is necessary to provide an alternative analysis of women's work that considers not only the production of capital, but also the production of society itself. Finally, situated in a field of social structures and grounded by specific laboring practices, one assumes a particular "standpoint." From this place, this standpoint, one both knows and acts.

Previous standpoint theorists concentrated on what women know as a result of what they do, with an emphasis on knowing. This knowledge, they claimed, gives women a unique view of the oppressive system and provides them an understanding of the whole system. Weeks points out, however, that such knowledge remains circumscribed within the oppressive system

11. Weeks, *Constituting Feminist Subjects*, 78.
12. Ibid., 82.
13. Ibid., 4ff.

What, Who, and How—The Real Meaning

and dilutes the acclaimed "uniqueness" of the standpoint. Knowledge hardly matters if women keep doing the same thing. As a result, Weeks is less interested in what we know and more intrigued by what we do, even while recognizing that each is a part of the same whole.

Since subjects are constructed within particular social orders, or contexts, we can understand the subject only by framing the order.[14] A significant part of the order involves gender and the roles that are assumed by those who self-identify with specific genders. As a role, gender cannot be discarded or replaced, but is one of the constitutive elements of the order. All of the social forces, inclusive of gender expectations, combine to produce the context. Some systems—sexism, for example—are so deeply embedded in our contemporary situations that they must be considered constitutive of the forces defining our context.

The contexts in which we find ourselves cannot be transformed in one sweeping movement. If this were possible, the Nineteenth Amendment to the Constitution of the United States would have guaranteed equality for women, and the Civil Rights Act of 1964 would have ended racism. Instead, our contexts represent a totality of practices with multiple fault lines where tremors and eruptions can occur. Internal relations between individuals within these formations are not predictable, but rather are open and contingent. The potential for change, then, rests with those situated both within and against the current structure. Thus, women, while historically and often currently occupying a place of oppression within church structures, also emerge through the cracks in the system as the renovators of the structure. Such "rebellion" can be traced back to the midwives in Egypt (Exod 1:15–21), who acted as agents of change while languishing under multiple systems of oppression—most notably race, class, and gender. The virgins and widows from the first decades of Christianity, before virginity was co-opted into "purity," who defied conventional marriage customs should also be considered renovators of the system. These are but two of many examples.

At the same time, subjects are not completely free to choose their own performance of gender norms but are compelled to reiterate and reproduce the norms that define their realities. Judith Butler labels this "ritualized production" and defines it as "a ritual reiterated under and through constraint, under and through the force of prohibition and taboo, with the threat of ostracism and even death controlling and compelling the shape of

---

14. Ibid., 70.

Feminine Registers

the production."[15] The girl who tries out for the high school football team may seem like a courageous maverick, but it is likely the boys on the team will not welcome her presence and the girls in the school will think she is oddly out of place. She may become a front-page headline, especially if she makes the team, but she will not have many friends with whom to share the excitement.

Challenging the norms can be more costly than the loss of friends, as Anne Hutchinson discovered when she suffered banishment and excommunication from Boston Colony because she "have rather bine a preacher than a Hearer."[16] More importantly, challenging the norms can never be a matter of simple choice because the one choosing is the product of the very norms she is challenging. At the same time, the one choosing is not locked into fatalistic structures, but continues to maintain the necessary agency to behave differently, even if only slightly. By suggesting that gender identity is established through ritualized production rather than by an intractable essence, Butler allows for the opportunity to offer variations on the rituals. Thus, while one is situated within a particular construction, the context of a worship service perhaps, one can still choose performances that either sustain or subvert the construction.

While Weeks agrees with the thrust of Butler's argument, she insists that the contexts determining gender performance and the effect of constant "engendering" are more powerful retardants to change than Butler is willing to admit.[17] Here, Weeks believes, standpoint theory offers a necessary correlation between the individual will to subvert the norms and the institutional forces restricting these choices. It is not enough to begin acting differently simply because one wants things to be different. Women as preachers must resist the constructing forces of social determinism by providing an alternative concept of feminine subjectivity.

Within an ecclesial setting these institutional forces are amplified by thousands of years of biblical interpretation, traditional patterns, and historical practice. The signifying practices that codify the inferiority of women are legion, and expelling these demons cannot be accomplished through one healing miracle. The relationship between these institutional factors and everyday practices compels behavior at the intersection of idea and institution. Weeks suggests the accumulated effect of these compulsory

15. Butler, *Bodies That Matter*, 95.
16. Hall, *Antimomian Controversy*, 382.
17. Weeks, *Constituting Feminist Subjects*, 133.

practices does produce a kind of naturalized or contingent necessity. Still, even though they produce a great deal of inertia and resistance to change, these contingencies are not intractable or determinative. The place where one participates in the practices that constitute one's context is also the place where one begins to fashion practices that will alter this context. Here, at a very basic level, is the one variable women as preachers must alter.

Claiming practices both past and present that affirm the work of women creates a context in which to reconstruct the lives of women in the church and the view of women as preachers. Since the experiences of women in the church have both positive and negative elements, this reconstruction will not be an uncritical celebration of all that women have been and done. Instead, the context will include selecting some practices from which to disengage and selecting other practices in which to engage.[18] Women stand within the context that defines their identity. From this place they cultivate the value-creating practices for women that subvert the dominant cultural context, and they desist from practicing that which they no longer want to be. Since direct opposition can easily be eliminated, Weeks suggests disengagement should involve negation from the inside of the system.[19] Women disengage from that which weakens their position and engage in that which strengthens it in order to cultivate an effective context for transformation. For example, for the women told repeatedly by the Southern Baptist Convention for the past three decades they cannot preach, such disengagement might be as simple as staying home from church. This response would likely have a deeper and more lasting effect on the life of their local churches than storming the pulpit.

Until recently, preaching was not a subject position typically occupied by women. Certainly women have preached for the past two millennia, but their paucity is evidenced in the reality that we can name so few of them. As a site for transformation, therefore, preaching is relatively new. If a woman attempts to shed her gender identity when occupying this site, however, transformational possibilities are limited. In such a scenario, the preaching site will always be a place for men, which is rarely and selectively opened to women. Women who occupy this place will be special individuals who have shed their culturally constructed feminine identity. In order for practices to change, both place and participants must acknowledge the totality of the gender construction. The fluidity of change, of course, cannot be clearly

18. Ibid., 145.
19. Ibid., 148.

tracked since it is both the place and the subjects who cause change in and for one other. Women alter the script by entering the preaching site, and the preaching event is gradually transformed as this place acknowledges and accepts their valid participation. A place that was formally "off-limits" to women gradually becomes not only a place that accepts women but also a place that expects and requires women. Certainly, it will be women as the "antagonistic subjects," to use Weeks' phrase, who cause this transformation, but the effects will be transformational for the entire register of preaching.

Tenor: Relationship—Who?

Sermon content and contextual location cannot be fully understood without a discussion of the communicators and the medium of their communication. Defining the relationship between the communicating parties helps diagnose the way gender shapes preaching by focusing on the interpersonal functions at work within the communication when a woman preaches. The relationship between the communicating parties, the conventions governing these relationships, and role of the parties within the communication are all part of this variable. When the preacher is a woman the relationships, the conventions, and the roles reflect the dynamics of those gendered expectations. As explained in the discussion of content and context, much of this information can be biased and partial because of the narratives dominating gendered cultural constructions. Knowing something about the relational categories that function beneath the surface of the communication provides a basis for naming some of the assumptions that govern how meanings are assigned to these relationships.

The systems routinely used to recite history, for example, can influence the relationship between communicating parties when gender roles within the church are defined through these historical perspectives. Consider that history is typically recited through wars, empires, or perhaps scientific discoveries, a dominating perspective. Other parts of history also tend to be narrated according to rivalries. The race to the moon is a prominent example of competition between empires occurring against the backdrop of a war in which no shots were fired. What we define as historically important will determine who is important historically. For most of human history, then, women were given subordinate roles simply by the way history is told. Women can easily find their place in this dominant delineation of history because it is their fathers, husbands, and sons who march off to war, reign as heads of state, and make important scientific discoveries; but there is little mention in the historical record of the women themselves. In these dominant accounts, men make history, and women relate to their history. Women preachers thus bear a version of history that occludes their contributions, scripts their characteristics, and marks their lives.

Such a rendition of history sets up a relationship between the woman preacher and the congregation that comes into conflict with an argument for equality. In 1792, when Mary Wollstonecraft published *A Vindication of the Rights of Woman*, she first had to deconstruct the reigning narratives that pronounced women unreasonable, irrational, and uneducable. Her claim was straightforward: women are what men expect them to be, often to the point of appearing ridiculous, because women must publicly agree with men in order to remain attractive to them.[20] The need to be attractive, according to Wollstonecraft, is exacerbated because men are notoriously unchaste, forcing women to be exceedingly attractive in order to keep them faithful. Thus, not only must a woman use her sexual wiles in order to "capture" a man who will marry her (agreeing with him no matter the unreasonableness of his claims) but she also must work diligently to retain him. Capturing and retaining a husband assumes the form of overindulgence on outward appearance without giving time and attention to the cultivation of her mind. Finally, for Wollstonecraft, only one solution is feasible. Men must rectify the situation because men have all the power. Over two hundred years later, magazine headlines, television sitcoms, and off-color jokes reveal that many of the concerns noted by Wollstonecraft continue to influence gendered performances and dominate the relational expectations for women.

By defining the performative characteristics of gender, Wollstonecraft anticipated later arguments about gender construction.[21] She argued that reason, virtue, and liberty are as important for the full development of women as they are for men because, at the core, men and women are the same. According to Wollstonecraft, such individual actualization for women would directly benefit men because they, too, would be freed from culturally defined behavior patterns. Her call to leave behind gender specificity and rise to the intellectual and rational heights all humans are

---

20. Wollstonecraft, *Vindication of the Rights of Women*, 129.

21. See de Beauvoir, *The Second Sex*; Butler, *Gender Trouble*; and more recently, Fausto-Sterling, *Sexing the Body*.

capable of reaching became a foundational claim of the women's suffrage movement, the first wave of feminism, and then again a generation later in the struggle for education reform and against discrimination in the workplace—the second wave. Riding the crest of the second wave, mainline denominations began instituting judicatory equality for women, setting up a host of relational dynamics for women who were caught between legislated equality and practiced inequality.

Equality has proven to be territory fraught with its own set of dangers. Obviously, all women are not equal across race, class, sexual orientation, etc. Claiming a core sameness, as did the liberal feminists beginning with Wollstonecraft, in an effort to enable women to thrive as individuals alongside men also strips women of some protective resources necessary for their well-being. Such sameness, furthermore, erases the distinctiveness women bring to the preaching event. The pressure to present sameness in order to approximate validity subsumes the differences in women's voices under an androcentric principle. The claim for difference is more nuanced than can be addressed by stirring in a few illustrations from the kitchen and calling it diverse. What women know is, admittedly, quite different from what men know, but how women know it provides the real distinction and captures one of the valuable contributions women can make to the proclamation of the gospel.

The research of Carol Gilligan, begun in 1982 with her book *In a Different Voice*, explored the importance of difference when considering a particular situation from a gendered perspective. Gilligan's research shows men and women experience the same situation differently based on their understanding of the relationship between self and others.[22] Women tend to focus on the relationship with those around them, including men, and men focus on themselves regardless of who may be around them. Whether this is an essential or constructed characteristic is beside the point. The important concept to recognize is that in human development, the dynamics of separation and attachment allow for the manifestation of different truths in the lives of men and women. For men, separation offers differentiation and empowerment through increased independence. For women, attachment provides sustenance and community through a continuous process of interdependence. Women find their identity in relationship with others, while men claim identity through individual achievement. This is not to say men do not form substantial relationships with others, but rather their

---

22. Gilligan, *In a Different Voice*, 156ff.

sense of self-worth is not as closely tied to these relationships as it is to their own accomplishments. Likewise, plenty of women derive self-worth from individual accomplishments, but the connection with others helps validate these achievements.

One hardly needs a degree in social psychology to consider how Gilligan's findings about relational differences affect the sermon when a woman preaches. From a negative perspective, traditional psychological theories scripting women as needy, emotional, and dependent (recall Wollstonecraft's protest against classifying women as "unreasonable, irrational, and uneducable") may be projected upon a woman who preaches, or even self-consciously assumed by her. Positively, however, the relational connectedness through which the preacher understands herself and by which she models communication can challenge conventional power differentials that elevate and celebrate the separate self.[23] From a theological perspective, the model of connectedness stresses the relationship between God and creation as opposed to the overzealous emphasis on personal salvation that has dominated so much of Western Christianity.

Gilligan wisely cautions, however, that these differences should be considered without ranking them so as not to reinforce stereotypical interpretations of gendered natures. As one scholar has noted, "'Special' may sound like superior, but it is also a euphemism for handicapped."[24] Employing the difference argument, therefore, is no less dangerous than playing the equality card. Women, lauded for their nurturing and relational capacities, can quickly find themselves relegated to stereotypical "helping" professions with no regard for their education or training in other arenas. Such gendered divisions of labor, as noted previously, can quickly erode the hard-won ground of pioneers like Wollstonecraft, the suffragists, and civil rights advocates. Gilligan's early research provides a valuable tool for beginning to understand these nuances and move the discussion beyond a simple "equal rights" declaration.

Recognizing and embracing differences between men and women helps militate against making sweeping generalizations, necessary since our "default" tendencies, even the tendencies of women, are to revert to conventional norms. As previously noted, people become what they are

---

23. Considerable work on the primacy of connection in women's lives is being done at the Stone Center's Jean Baker Miller Training Institute at Wellesley College. See especially Jordan et al., *Women's Growth in Connection*; Jordan, *Women's Growth in Diversity*; and Jordan et al., *The Complexity of Connection*.

24. Faludi, "Carol Gilligan: Different Voices or Victorian Echoes?" 327.

Feminine Registers

expected to be. Individuals are "always-already" subjects of the ideology that defines them, making them "abstract" as individuals. Even while such ideological understandings operate contextually, they also determine and define interpersonal definitions. Equality and difference are relational categories operating between the preacher and the congregation, and the lens through which each of the communicating parties views the other has implications for the meaning of the sermon.

Consider the annual occasion of inviting a woman to preach, typical in several mainline churches, under the guise of something like "Women in the Pulpit Sunday."[25] Having played this part several times, I can attest that more attention will be paid to how I look than to what I say. Certainly, congregants are appreciative when they hear a good sermon—leaving aside for a moment the relative definition of good. A good sermon, however, is not necessary in order to validate the experience of having had a woman in the pulpit to look at for a bit. Post-worship handshaking rituals are sprinkled with comments from women related to hairstyle and complexion, while men offer more robust remarks such as, "You sure are better looking than our regular preacher."[26]

This habit does not so much belie prejudice or superficiality on their part as it reflects a cultural reality—in a world of desires, women occupy the category of the desired, and men do the desiring. Men and women alike, therefore, offer assessments of this dominant relational criterion before moving on to observe other characteristics of the woman before them, such as whether she can preach or not. The woman who would preach, particularly on a day laden with such a problematic descriptor as "women in the pulpit," is predefined by the gender ideologies swirling around the very subject of women. She participates in the ongoing construction of the site, styling her hair and carefully attending to facial characteristics, even while she is constituted by it.

---

25. Recognized annually in South Carolina, this day comes with an assortment of worship aids that include scripture suggestions, hymn selection, an annual theme, and obviously the expectation that a woman will be invited to preach. See http://www.umcsc.org/home/ai1ec_event/women-in-the-pulpit-sunday-2/?instance_id=.

26. Following worship in a church where I had appeared as the guest preacher, one elderly man took my hand and declared, "You have mighty pretty feet" (McMannen United Methodist Church, Durham, North Carolina, April 27, 2008). By telling this story I am not implying that parishioners never make assessments about body image when the preacher is a man, but physical appearance does not tend to be the dominant characteristic upon which they fixate in quite the same way.

When women assume more permanent roles beyond annual guest preacher, they often do so under the guise of cultural feminine norms such as nurturing and mothering. These norms also come bearing particular characteristics that define relationships. Indeed, some of those who early on championed having women move into more visible leadership roles in the church offered as incentive the goal of making the pastorate more nurturing.[27] Claiming women are the "best" nurturers soon morphs into the belief that women are *only* nurturers. The reduction of women to "nurturers" then circumscribes the roles they should assume as preachers, and the relationship they offer for the preaching event is only valuable in so far as it fits this description. A woman who does not fit this culturally prescribed role strikes a dissonant chord for the listeners, who have been conditioned by particular relational expectations.

Furthermore, promoting the presence of women because of their "nurturing nature" encourages women to fill the roles scripted for them, as mentioned previously. The repercussions for such scripting reinforce many of the discoveries made by Leslie Salzinger, *Genders in Production*, who claims, "symbolizing practices, structures of meaning, and situated intentions shape managerial decisions."[28] Each of these criteria just as readily shape the expectations of the church members who also regularly participate in their own symbolizing practices, structures of meaning, and situated intentions. Althusser reminds us that people become what they are expected to be; Salzinger takes this thought one step further and suggests that individuals can be "produced" within the settings where they exist. By linking conventional gender roles with expectations about the preacher, congregations whose image of women is nurturing can actually produce women who imagine themselves as nurturers. While nurture is one of the basic tenets of ministry regularly practiced through pastoral care and worship leadership, to reduce the contributions of women to nurture, or any other single category, is to nullify the multiple qualities women bring to ministry and preaching.

Gendered divisions of labor play a crucial role in defining the relational categories operating when a woman preaches. The challenge, then,

---

27. Lehman, "Women's Path into Ministry," 28–30.

28. Salzinger, *Genders in Production*, 159. Salzinger's ethnographic work focuses on factory workers in Mexico and describes a variety of settings in which workers not only become what they are expected to be (Althusser), but are produced through the discursive processes of the workplace. It does not require much imagination to see how her conclusions are applicable to the church.

is not to replicate the culturally naturalized relational models or succumb to uniformly romanticized ideals, but for women to become active subjects capable of transforming the subject position itself through social change. If social phenomena are the products of multiple determinants, then gender identity as one such phenomenon both determines and is determined by a constellation of factors, each of which impacts gender identity in specific ways. The laboring practices imposed by these categories can become a site for change when the laboring practices of women are viewed as valuable to the field of homiletics. Focusing on the desires, values, and needs exposed through gendered divisions of labor allows for an honest assessment of contributions made by women.

Obviously, the relationships operating in a sermon are substantially influenced by these structures of meaning when a woman preaches. Sermons are produced and proclaimed while projecting the cultural attendants for "woman" against a constant barrage of images relegating women to secondary roles. These images include God the Father, His only Son, kingdom of Heaven, Son of Man, etc. Degrees of subjectivity and subjection are manifest in the contextual norms of the discourse, and these implied subject positions are often locked into implied structures of meaning. Levels of meaning are both assumed and reproduced by the ones engaged in the discourse, and shedding these default gender categories requires more than satisfying quotas.

Sermons, as theological constructions and scriptural expositions, provide a means for truth-telling that enable the worshiping public to see and hear different kinds of relationships. The congregation as a public is called to hear and respond to the otherness of the voices in their midst as well as the otherness made possible by the hope of God's presence in their midst. New voices add new pieces to the story, enriching the meaning-making possibilities for those in the center as well as those on the margins. What had once been a relationship of inequality—men preach, women listen—becomes a relationship of mutuality. Men and women preach; men and women listen. Each, however, tells the story differently, enabling those who listen to hear new possibilities for their own lives. With new voices offering new words about what has happened, shaping the identity of all who hear them, a different relationship starts to form that is neither circumscribed by singular gender expectations nor obscured by androgynous equality claims.

What, Who, and How—The Real Meaning

Mode: Method—How?

In spite of our linear discussion, register variables do not occur sequentially, building up the meaning of a particular communication as we diagnose each component. Each variable affects the meaning of a discourse even if, under certain conditions, some variables exert more influence in some situations than in others. Content is often considered the dominant meaning-making variable for preaching, a sort of first impression, but this need not be the case. How one preaches might just as readily offer the first impression around which the other variables orbit. Consider the occasion of driving a long distance, losing the radio signal, and twisting the dial in search of a new station. After hearing only seconds of the broadcast we can determine a great deal about its type by how it sounds. A sportscaster offering commentary between batters in a baseball game readily connects us to the event, and even if we might not instantly recognize the voice as one belonging to a baseball game, we are likely to make the connection to some sporting event. Weather reports, headline news, musical reviews, even the music begin to impart meaning on the basis of how we hear them. If we know anything at all about preaching, we know how a radio preacher sounds. We need not be sitting in a pew or see him standing at the pulpit to know we are listening to a sermon. Thus, while mode rounds out this discussion of meaning-making possibilities, its importance for the meaning of the sermon is no less integral to the whole.

How we hear packs as much freight into the meaning as where we are and who is communicating. While sermons are most often spoken, not sung or mimed (though either of those might work), a host of possibilities exist within this semiotic medium. These semiotic possibilities have much to do with tone, tempo, and timbre, and reviewing a public speaking manual can explain how these ingredients affect voice clarity and make distinctions between the voices of men and women. When a woman delivers the sermon, however, her embodied presence will impart meaning to the preaching event through both the speaking and the hearing before she ever utters the first word. Questions about authority addressed in the first chapter and further examined through the discussions of context and relationship arise again in relation to how sermons are preached. Does this "body" have a right to preach? Gendered expectations about power and submission, again scripted through hundreds of years of textual interpretation and traditional conditioning, are foregrounded by questions of

Feminine Registers

"how?" Why is this woman shouting, crying, laughing? How sermons are spoken aloud helps name these anticipated categories and further reveals the meaning-making systems working within them.

Some basic differences between how men and women preach can be seen by analyzing a set of sermons on the basis of form, text, theme, and purpose.[29] The results are not dramatic, but substantive enough to show particular tendencies women bring to the preaching event, all the while remembering that what preachers communicate cannot be separated from how they communicate it. The analysis shows women are reluctant to criticize the church while men are reluctant to offer a personal testimony. Nearly half the women in the sample offered personal testimony, and over half of the men were critical of the church and society. Other matters such as interpreting scripture, teaching, exhorting, and exegeting are important to both men and women, though in varying degrees. For instance, all the sermons by women involved the homiletical task of interpreting scripture, but more than 10 percent of the men omitted this content. Nearly twice as many women as men provided exegetical information in their sermons. On the other hand, the sermons of slightly more men than women involved teaching.

Focusing on these two areas where the sermons of men and women differ most markedly suggests, in a general sense, that women appear to use more personal stories and men tend to focus on addressing external issues. This finding reflects the research of Carol Gilligan discussed earlier. Who preachers understand themselves to be relationally coincides with how they chose to communicate. And, of course, decisions about how to communicate will influence the material used by the preacher for proclamation.

This kind of analysis is not difficult to plot. A more subtle distinction about how women preach centers on her physical body. Since bodies cannot be excluded from an analysis of any oral communication, and especially not from preaching, a study of preaching must incorporate the body's real presence in the pulpit. To deny the presence of a gendered body is to perpetuate the bifurcation of the human being into polarized categories of mind and body, reason and passion, psychology and biology, sense and sensibility, self and other, transcendence and immanence, etc. Such thinking necessarily ranks the terms so that the suppressed term becomes the objective through which its counterpart is privileged. As pointed out earlier in Chopp's discussion of two-tier language systems, such privileging cannot

---

29. Sanders, "Woman as Preacher," 211.

exist without the subordination and negation of the other. Thus, in this kind of dualism, body represents what mind is not, with mind occupying the place of value. Legions of scholars have already shown how "woman" occupies the subordinate categories that grant validity to "man" by representing what man is not. No one, however, whether male or female, stands in the pulpit as a bodiless mind.

Three systems proceeding from dualism tend to dominate our contemporary concepts of the body.[30] In the first, the body is treated as an organic system of interrelated parts studied for how it is impacted by sensation, epistemology, and culture. The goal in this approach is to scrutinize objectively the body's sensations and activities through the higher facilities of mind and reason. Such an approach ignores the reality that organic bodies both construct and are constructed by an interior consciousness and perspective. Another dualistic classification identifies the body as a vessel filled with consciousness, possessed by an animating subjectivity, but with no agency of its own. As an instrument the body is conditioned or constructed to occupy a particular category, but the body itself is passive in this construction. In the last configuration, the body becomes the signifying medium for expressing the interior sense of one's self even as it serves as the conduit for receiving information from the external world. Here again, the body is fundamentally passive, bearing information that comes from elsewhere, a sort of permeable intermediary.

In each of these systems corporeality remains a secondary, and often undesirable, inevitability in the acquisition of knowledge and understanding. Bodies, however, cannot be objectively understood as though the body itself does not participate in the social construction of its own definition. No body exists without its historical, social, and cultural representations. As the locus for perspective and agency, action and reaction, bodies function as objects that contain themselves subjectively. A false divide between the psychic interior and the corporeal exterior only serves to reify universal humanity at the expense of sexually specific bodies. One does not have a body the way one possesses other objects; one is a body, and this body fully participates in the preaching event.

Christianity has long championed the position that a person is both body and soul, one being related to God, indivisible. Writing in the midst of Neoplatonist philosophies, Paul and later Augustine clearly depict the unity of the person over and against platonic dualism. For Augustine, the

---

30. Grosz, *Volatile Bodies*, 8f.

description of the person extends beyond the polemical notion of matter versus spirit, analogous to Cartesian dualisms of body versus soul, that lead us finally to simplistic definitions of bad versus good.[31] Christianity avows that the body and the soul together are condemned through sin, and the body and the soul together are redeemed by grace. For Augustine, while the body never becomes soul nor the soul a body, both body and soul are essential elements in order for personhood to exist.[32] The soul that comes from God along with the body formed by God unite to create the person. When that person preaches, she brings her whole self into the pulpit.

One way for a congregation to understand the body of a woman preacher is by invoking a gender neutral, "one in Christ" interpretation. Mimicking Paul's instruction to the Galatians—". . . there is no longer male and female; for all of you are one in Christ Jesus" (Gal 3:28)—they attempt to view her in gender-neutral ways that emphasize the transcendent nature of Christianity. Obviously, Paul was urging the Galatians to accept one another without qualification, but his words also move toward a universalizing claim of "least common denominator."[33] The former concept for women as preachers seems reasonable, but the latter thinking has the disadvantage of masking the distinctiveness of women's particularities in order to make them acceptable as preachers. The universal or transcendent human continues to project a masculine image that replicates itself as the norm and disallows a self-representation of the specifically feminine. In this project, the less the preacher looks and acts like a woman, the better the situation. Even if she does not necessarily act like a man, she would do well to lay aside overtly feminine attributes, like dangling earrings. These gendered attributes are further compounded by clerical modes of dress, especially since preachers, typically men, have insisted on donning long flowing robes, typically worn by women.

True gender neutrality, even if it could be achieved, denies the corporeal existence of the one doing the preaching. Because the preacher is not amorphous, a mouth without a body, the specificity of the body has implications for the reception of the gospel. Instead of reacting against negative stereotypes about women by developing equalizing or neutralizing

---

31. Fredriksen, "Beyond the Body/Soul Dichotomy," 113.

32. Portailié, *Guide to the Thought of Augustine*, 146.

33. In attempting to convince ourselves that the gender or the race of the preacher "do not matter," we are only calling attention to the fact that we know there is a difference. Paul had high hopes for the Galatians that might not be possible this side of the eschaton.

strategies that deny their existence, a more authentic response involves claiming the gendered body along with all the cultural and religious constructions presented by it, including dangling earrings. Such a task begins with an honest assessment of the gender constructions projected upon a female preacher by the congregation.

The preacher's body is one more interpretive variable used by the congregation to impart meaning to the sermon, so how the congregants read her body will affect the sermon. Feminist theory offers several ways to discuss the body. The most pervasive theory, essentialism, is latent in nearly all our assumptions about gendered bodies, even as we struggle to deconstruct gender stereotypes. Essentialists concentrate on the biological differences between men and women by using sexual binaries. By privileging certain attributes, such as nurturing and negotiating, as essential to women, they hope to claim credibility for the work and worth of women throughout the world. One hears echoes of this thinking in comments such as the following: "If women ran the world there would be no more wars." The naivety of this comment, though seemingly complimentary to women, masks a form of dualistic thinking that continues to view a woman primarily for what she is not. Leaving aside the problem of war in the first place, a woman is not brave enough, strong enough, or clever enough to win a war, so why would she start one? Many congregations continue to languish under the residual fallout of dualistic thinking, seeing a female preacher foremost for what she is not. Attempts to define what she is positively—nurturing, for instance—create a different set of dilemmas, as previously noted. Scholars such as Rosemary Radford Ruether and Mary Daly have long pointed out that dualistic thinking casts women as "the other," the lower half of a binary opposite. This contributes to a host of exclusionary practices, including the exclusion of women from religious leadership. Just as dualism leaves us with a bifurcated person, sexual binaries leave us with a bifurcated humanity.

Social construction is another dominant feminist theory that informs how the body of the preacher imparts meaning to the sermon. According to constructivists, the aforementioned "essentials" are culturally imposed conventions masquerading as authentic feminine characteristics. For example, women have been constructed as relational and nurturing because they have always stayed home "relating to and nurturing" the children. Given the alternative of waging war, building empires, and dominating opponents, women could just as readily excel as men have. The more extreme constructivists claim that "culture so profoundly determines human beings that no point beyond convention exists from which to ascertain what is 'nature' with respect to sexual difference."[34] Or as Simone de Beauvoir has opined, "one is not born a woman, but, rather, becomes one."[35] For constructivists, gender is not correlated with sexual difference. Constructivists offer, by way of example, a hypothetical world where hair color is the determinative lens through which people are viewed. This world, of course, is not hypothetical at all when hair becomes skin, as people of color can readily attest. "Elaborate and seemingly hypothetical apparatuses for evaluating the significance of color"[36] have been in place for millennia. If this point can be admitted, it is not a great leap to confirm that cultural/gender constructs skew our vision and distort our hearing. Here again, how the congregation constructs the body of the one occupying the pulpit has bearing on how they hear what she has to say.

The essentialist and constructivist theories help explain some of the preconceived notions that follow women into the pulpit; however, neither definition fully captures the multifaceted differences between men and women. Essentialism offers the benefit of recognizing the distinctive gifts of women, but includes the danger these distinctions will be employed as additional tools of exclusion. Furthermore, extreme essentialism succumbs to its own trap by reifying feminine attributes by denigrating masculine traits. Here women's ways are not so much the equal of men's as they are superior to them; nurture is not as good as power, it is better. Thus, essentialism trades one absolute for another without any room for particularity.

On the other hand, while constructivism recognizes the cultural production of gender that often begins before birth, it ignores the body's physical presence—male and female bodies are different, and some of these fundamental differences are built into the fabric of creation. While bodies are not fixed by genetic or biological materiality, neither is sexual difference only a matter of inscription and codification. Ideas and attitudes toward the body influence the functions of the body itself, contributing to its possibilities and its limitations. Actions that seemed impossible for a body to undertake at a given time or in a given place are readily possible in other times and places. A hundred years ago women could not vote for the president of the United States, let alone run for the office. On the other hand, bodies do have very real limits; so far the human body cannot fly without

---

34. Butler, *Gender Trouble*, 35.

35. de Beauvoir, *Second Sex*, 301.

36. Jones, *Feminist Theory and Christian Theology*, 35

the aid of mechanical devices. Still, even biological constraints that seemed inviolable only a few years ago can become blurred. Birth control and artificial insemination each contribute from opposite places to complicating the biological definition of woman as mother. As it turns out, all women are not mothers, and some are not because they do not want to be.

The challenge is to wrest corporeality away from the constraints that have polarized it through oppositional categories. In response to these oppositional theories, several designations have emerged that blend elements from both theories. Certainly, Carol Gilligan's research helps shift the focus to the different experiences for men and women in the relationship between self and others without making either of them essential.[37] Bodies are not one of many variations underlying humanity; they are integral to humanity itself. Rather than representing one half of a binary pair, the body should serve as a border between the private and the public, the self and the other. Likewise, one particular body does not represent the ideal norm (straight white males in the West, for example) against which all other bodies are valued, but the variety and richness of multiple body types must be celebrated and encouraged.

Gendered perceptions of the body both inform and challenge how the sermon is heard. Furthermore, bodies can be adapted to specific situations according to the performance required. Whether they are male or female, day care workers can nurture and army privates can lock and load. Men and women can preach. When women do preach, the subject of their physical body becomes an integral variable to the meaning-making possibilities of the sermon. To deny the corporeal presence of the bodies we have is to refuse the revelatory power offered to us by God.

Women should speak from our church's pulpits, not by disguising their voices as generic and assuming essentialist femininity, but by proclaiming the truth of their own experiences. All proclamation is refracted through and hybridized by the structures around it—economic, cultural, political, and theological. Sermons are not immune to these influences. Indeed, if they were, preaching would be a useless exercise of self-indulgence. The experiences of preachers refracted through the structures around them grant validity to the proclamation by connecting it to the concrete world where faith is lived and proclaimed. The language used by the preacher functions in concert with all of these structures as they are known by the congregation. When a woman occupies the preaching space of a particular

---

37. Gilligan, *In a Different Voice*, 156.

community of faith, she brings her own associations into the space, adding another dimension to the structures lived and known within that gathered community.

Each register shift opens up new possibilities for meaning. Placing women in the position of power and authority, the pulpit, alters the context. Expanding relational possibilities by inviting an assortment of voices influences the communicating parties. Listening to the body before us, a woman, changes how we hear. Each register shift offers the possibility for deeper and fuller ways of hearing the gospel and provides enrichment for the entire community.

4

Sermon Registers at Work

Every preacher can tell stories about hearing phrases from a sermon repeated on the front steps after worship or in the coffee shop on Monday morning, with accompanying interpretations that never occurred to us when the words poured forth on Sunday morning. Fortunate indeed is the preacher who is first asked, "What did you mean by . . . ?" before the congregational redactors begin holding forth with their own renditions. When the word is proclaimed, the one preaching loses control. Rebecca Chopp suggests this happens because there is "space between our meaning and our proclaiming."[1] The discussion about register demonstrates that what moves into this space comes into focus through the variables surrounding the communicating parties. Certain meanings will never occur at all and some meanings will always be readily apparent. The adventure in preaching lies between the poles of "impossible" and "of course," and the challenge for women is to occupy this ground without their proclamation being rejected as preposterous or taken for granted dismissively.

To further demonstrate the importance of women's voices we need to identify those places where scripture and church tradition presume either rejection or acceptance of women and, thus, shape the proclamation of women, sometimes before a word is ever spoken. Gender influences each variable—the content, the relationship, and the medium—but the individual effect of gender on each intersection radiates through the entire communication.

---

1. Chopp, *Power to Speak*, 65.

Because scripture and tradition, providing sermon content, are such dominant components in preaching, they can overshadow the relationship between the communicating parties and the form of communication unless some conventional assumptions about them are challenged. Even while Christianity did not invent patriarchy and has sometimes defended women against some of the worst forms of misogyny, it remains the case that the Bible is regularly invoked to support gender hierarchies and is used by many church polities to discourage the full inclusion of women. Some of these issues occur because of mistranslation and misinterpretation, but other matters are integral to the text and tradition themselves. For example, Elizabeth Schüssler Fiorenza points out that the Bible often fails to supply women with the liberating texts that are readily available for the poor and the sojourner. Rather than emancipating women, the Bible is, quite often, at the root of the problem.[2]

When considering the meaning-making possibilities of a sermon, numerous scholars attentive to this reading regime for scripture can cite places where the text demonizes women, degrades female sexuality, minimizes women's experiences, and erases women from salvation history. Thus, scripture cannot be read simply as a text of liberation for women by searching for a "canon within a canon," but must itself be liberated from its own complicity in the oppression of women. Content, however, never operates in isolation. The relationships pre-formed by the content of scripture and scripted through centuries of interpretation also inform the obstacles faced by women as preachers.

Using the building blocks of ideological criticism, feminist scholars begin with the assumption that the text and tradition are not neutral, nor are its interpreters objective. These ideological biases limit the communication possibilities and affect the interpersonal potential because much of what is found in scripture regarding women is more prescriptive than descriptive. The prescriptions about women control how sermons are heard because how we listen is circumscribed by the text and the interpreters. In other words, the portrayal of women in the text will correspond more closely to an androcentric understanding of the role of women instead of providing an accurate rendition of their lives. The misrepresentation is reinforced when the majority of the interpreters of the biblical tradition are also men sharing the mindset of those who produced the text. Such interpreters are not predisposed to notice anything amiss in the portrayal of women by the

---

2. Schüssler Fiorenza, *In Memory of Her*, 31.

text or within the tradition, similar to Farley's middle axioms, because the norms have established the expectations, bringing the matter around again to the preposterous or the obvious.

The crux of the matter goes far beyond sharing preaching opportunities with women because it is a nice thing to do. The matter strikes at the very essence of God's revelation to humanity and God's demonstration of grace within creation. When the revelation is truncated through exclusion and the demonstration is segmented by devaluation, it is not only the excluded women or the exalted men who suffer the loss. The fullness of God's presence in our lives fails to materialize. As church practices and, in some traditions, official policies continue to vacillate between the acceptance and rejection of women as preachers based, in large part, on tired arguments, the concept of register offers a fresh analysis to help consider their importance for preaching. New interpretations of the text and tradition that name God's presence among us grant new meaning to the word that is born again each time a person rises to proclaim it. A God who is greater than all our imaginative possibilities can only be honored when we declare all the possibilities imaginable.

Meanings Beneath the Surface

Knowing something about one of the register variables allows us to deduce certain attributes about the other variables, which can lead to an assumption about the meaning of the communication. One variable is not always enough information, however, to make an accurate prediction about the possibilities for meaning in a particular situation. A simple class exercise conducted by Stanley Fish demonstrates this claim.[3] Students in his contemporary poetry class entered the classroom and noticed a "poem" already written on the board. With his encouragement they launched into a lively discussion of this composition, using the appropriate diagnostic tools to debate the inherent meaning of the collection of words before them. Shortly before the end of the class period, Fish informed the students that the "poem" on the board before them was really an assignment for the previous class around which he had drawn a box before the current class entered the room. He then congratulated them on their predictable performance and dismissed class.

---

3. Fish, "How to Recognize a Poem," 322ff.

While the students' discussion ensued, in large part, on the basis of expectation—poetry students expect to talk about poetry—accurate interpretations are possible only when all three register variables are coherent. The professor, dictating the relational variable, created the misinterpretation by encouraging the students to discuss the poetic merits of nothing more than a class assignment. While Fish did somewhat mislead his students by setting up an artificial situation, the results of his experiment demonstrate the interdependence of each of the register variables to determine understandings. Knowing the context—poetry class—did not enable an accurate prediction of the meaning of the information on the board. How Fish communicated, as the authority figure in the class, affected the content on the board. The content was then made into something by the communicating parties that it was never intended to be. This exercise demonstrates the interdependence of the three register variables. Changing one variable changes the meaning.

Beyond Fish's ability to manufacture interesting classroom experiments, his work is integral for understanding the meaning-making potential of a discourse. The classroom experiment performed on his poetry students proves the more salient point that interpretation is as much the work of constructing as it is the work of construing. The students in his class "made" a poem out of the words on the board even when no such understanding existed for those words prior to their arrival in the classroom. The students, however, never could have talked about the words on the board as poetry without a working knowledge of poetry as a literary form. Students and professor shared a common understanding of poetry and similar expectations about the necessary ingredients for a discussion of poetry. The point is that individuals do not create meaning out of nothing, nor does the text contain an inherent meaning separate from the interpretive community. Meanings are "given" to them by the communities, and the possibility for understanding between participants comes from a shared set of understandings: "a way of thinking, a form of life, shares us, and implicates us in a world of already-in-place objects, purposes, goals, procedures, values, and so on . . ."[4]

Like the students in Fish's poetry class, the congregation and the preacher share and are shared by a way of thinking, a form of life. The sermon may act as a communicative medium between them, but they each, congregation and preacher, bring their own understanding of a sermon

---

4. Fish, "Is There a Text in This Class?" 304.

to the preaching event just as they bring an expectation about who will deliver the sermon. Nevertheless, the sermon exists in a sea of instability and indeterminate meaning as language is appropriated by those engaged in the communicative process. Consider the conversation between Jesus and Nicodemus as recorded in the Gospel of John (3:1–10). After paying Jesus the requisite compliment to get the conversation started, Nicodemus makes a reference to God's presence. Jesus then utters the now infamous words, "Very truly, I tell you, no one can see the kingdom of God without being born from above." Or is it "born again"? The Greek word *anōthen* provides the ambiguity that is unresolved by the English translations. Jesus seems to have intended for the statement to communicate a transformation of one's viewpoint in order to comprehend God's presence in the world, a form of rebirth. Nicodemus heard rebirth and thought of wombs, labor, and infancy. Either definition of *anōthen* is correct and both definitions are derived from an interpretive system shared by Jesus and Nicodemus. They share common assumptions about God's reign and about birthing practices that enable them to communicate with one another. The instability of the communication arises because of the indeterminate meaning of the word *anōthen*. The instability and indeterminateness do not represent infinite possibilities because the words are embedded in a particular situation that contains their meaning.[5] The multiple meanings for *anōthen* do not arise after Jesus speaks the word, but are already present in the potential ways the word could be heard by Nicodemus.

As determinants of language, the variables—content/context, relationship, and method—predict the meanings conveyed by the words. They make explicit a particular understanding, not from the words themselves, but from the situation that contains the words, the ones participating in the situation, and the way the words are presented. With only limited information, individuals will construct meanings based on their most common experiences. So, for Nicodemus, having never thought of birth as anything other than carnal, the idea of new birth or new life coming through God's spirit never occurred to him. Such a novel concept must be introduced to him from outside the categories that normally circumscribe his world, but the potential for such an understanding is already present in the possible ways Nicodemus might hear *anōthen*. If not, then the conversation between Jesus and Nicodemus would break down completely.

---

5. Ibid., 307.

Opponents of this methodology will insist that words do have meaning independent of their situations and that meaning is brought to the situation when the word is invoked. One hears a word and then attaches the appropriate meaning to it. Certainly, individuals must regularly make determinations about meaning from within their situations, just as Nicodemus had to determine what Jesus meant by *anōthen* by hearing more about it from Jesus. But the meaning of the word *anōthen* is being made in the course of the conversation between Nicodemus and Jesus in the same manner that Fish's students made a poem out of a column of words left on the board from a previous class. Deferring to the obvious, as the students and Nicodemus learned, does not necessarily produce the correct understanding.

According to Fish, even these obvious meanings arise through an association with what is typical. What is typical or normal, of course, is nothing more than what is expected, and without additional information listeners will revert to the most obvious meaning. Conflating normal with what is "natural" creates the same traps for misunderstanding. For example, in our society a child naturally receives the surname of his or her father at birth and a girl typically assumes the surname of her husband upon marriage. Children who do not receive the father's surname occupy categories that require additional explanation, often burdened by negative stereotypes, and a woman who retains her father's name rather than assuming her husband's name continues to raise an eyebrow in our society. We live in a patrilineal culture that imposes definitions of natural on our naming practices.

The Mosou people of southwest China live in a matrilineal culture.[6] Children trace their heritage and maintain their identity through their mothers. The most dominant male figures in the lives of these children are their uncles, not their fathers, though children are usually well aware of the paternal biological connections. Because of the matrilineal convention, brothers remain closely related to their sisters through their mothers. For a child to carry the father's surname in this society would require additional explanation, possibly burdened by negative stereotypes, and for a woman to assume the name of her male partner could not happen. What seems natural to us within our societal construct turns out to be only contextual. Still, because patrilineal societies dominate our culture, the Mosou people fascinate us.

---

6. See *The Women's Kingdom*, a short film by Chinese journalist Xiaoli Zhou.

We can, however, begin to understand this different familial configuration because of several determinate meanings that we share with the Mosou people. Without any common categories between our cultures, the Mosou would be incomprehensible to us. The presence of shared determinate meanings allows us to expand our categories of understanding precisely because we can incorporate information that comes from outside our current configurations. In this example, both matrilineal and patrilineal societies share an understanding of biological progeny, and the makeup of the family unit is based on these biological relationships—DNA connects us. In neither society is care of children limited exclusively to direct offspring and not even necessarily to children biologically related to the adult who provides care, even while such relationships do heighten the expectation of responsibility. From this baseline understanding the conversation progresses by incorporating ways of thinking that expand the previous horizons for family configuration. While it is not likely that Americans will suddenly throw over patrilineal nomenclature, to say nothing of the patrimonial laws that permeate our entire understanding of what is "mine," it is entertaining to consider what my home would feel like if my maternal uncle and my brother were the primary male figures in the lives of my own children. But I can only imagine this because I first know something about families.

So it is that we haltingly and gradually change the way we think. The pace at which we make this change depends on the proportion of shared meanings. Consider the views of feminist theorist Shulamith Firestone, a Canadian born, American educated, white middleclass woman, who "looks like us" in almost every way. Firestone disparages the notion of any biological connection between parents and children because of her foundational premise that "the biological family is an inherently unequal power distribution."[7] Firestone asserts that even the woman who achieves equality in every way with her husband—education, salary, etc.—will find "when she bears children and takes care of infants, she is once again totally incapacitated."[8] Optimistic about the possibilities for reproduction through cybernetics, Firestone proposes that reproduction of the species should not be the sole responsibility of one sex for the benefit of both and that half-hearted efforts to reform society by providing appropriate maternity

---

7. Firestone, *Dialectic of Sex*, 9.
8. Ibid., 44.

or family leave shored up by adequate childcare options only perpetuate the problem by placating women in the midst of their maternal crises.[9]

Of course, Firestone's utopia necessarily includes those who wish to bear children, but she predicts that within only a few generations[10] no women will choose such a "temporary deformation of the body of the individual for the sake of the species."[11] Those who voluntarily choose such work—women for the bearing, and women and men for the rearing—should be adequately compensated for their roles and all provisions for the care of the children should be made available to them. The rest of us, even those of us who inadvertently bear children, will be allowed to pursue our own lives without responsibility for or claim on our biological progeny. We would, however, be expected to support financially and materially those individuals who make children their priority in a manner not dissimilar to our support of those individuals who defend "liberty and justice for all" while we work and play in the oblivion of freedom.

Even though we hold fewer societal and cultural meanings in common with the Mosou people than with Firestone, her notion of familial configuration is more "foreign" to our way of thinking. Shulamith Firestone makes the Mosou people sound more "normal" by the minute. Even so, the ability to comprehend Firestone's argument is grounded in several shared determinate meanings, not the least of which is that any woman who has birthed a child knows it will slow her down for a few days. Whether or not we agree with Firestone's solution to the "inherently unequal power distribution," we can enter the conversation because we are all products of biological families and some of us produce them as well. We have, to use Fish's terminology, a "pretext" for family when we enter the conversation with Firestone. Consequently, comprehending and appreciating Firestone's argument depends on how attached we are to our pretext, our conventional notions of family, and not on whether we know how babies are made.

The concept of pretext is critical for understanding how register captures the meaning-making process of preaching. Each variable is weighted with pretext, so much so in some instances that no new meanings can penetrate through the layers. "Women should be silent in the churches" (1 Cor 14:34) is a conversation-stopper, and changing one's opinion about the legitimacy of women speaking in church requires more than simply

---

9. Ibid., 185.
10. Ibid., 205–6.
11. Ibid., 180.

hearing a woman preach a "good" sermon. Such modification might start with hearing a good sermon, but even the definition of what constitutes "good" will be constrained by the more immediate concern already in place—in this particular instance, women should be silent in the churches. In other words, the sermon is perceived within a structure of norms about who speaks and who is silent.[12] Revising one's attitude toward women as preachers requires modification of the norms, dare we say prejudices, which are already in place. When such modification begins to occur, new voices can bring forth different, but faithful, proclamations.

Register of a Sermon

Registers have both macro meanings and micro meanings. In other words, at the macro level, when we think of a sermon we think of a particular form of communication: "the delivering of a religious discourse by a preacher to an audience."[13] As previously discussed, "woman" as a subject position affects each of the register variables of the sermon at the macro level when she preaches. Preconceived expectations related to social location, gender construction, and language operation each shift in concert with the degree of difference she represents in the communication event. Because these categories are only temporarily stable, her presence intersects with the constellation of meanings generated through them and adds a new interpretive possibility to each variable.

Likewise, the sermon as a liturgical component elicits certain expectations from people that can even be incorporated into non-liturgical circumstances. When my children mutter, "Here comes another sermon," they are not referencing their presence in a worship service during which I will deliver the sermon. They are referencing the scolding they are about to receive related to the dirty laundry on their bedroom floor or the dirty dishes piled in the sink. While my criticism of their household hygiene bears little resemblance to the proclamation of the word offered during a worship service, the meaning of the declaration is related to a specific type of communication: one person speaking authoritatively to another who, for the most part, is not encouraged to contribute to the declaration because the speaking party provides all the necessary information for the communication event, inclusive of value statements and ultimatums. In

12. Fish, "Is There a Text in This Class?" 318.
13. Kienzle and Walker, *Women Preachers and Prophets*, xiv.

the example of my children, I am the one who evaluates the cleanliness of the bedroom floor or the kitchen sink and I am the one who pronounces the outcome of this condition. The context has shifted entirely since my kitchen bears no resemblance to a sanctuary, but the register has changed very little because the relationship hierarchy and communication method remain constant. The propensity of my children to identify my instruction as a sermon is facilitated less by the fact that I am a preacher and more by their familiarity with sermons heard in worship. Their experience of a sermon is hearing one person, the preacher, evaluate the condition of some others, the congregation, and offer a resolution gleaned from the factors that influence the situation.

The macro meaning of a sermon hinges on these broad categorical expectations of preaching, at least for those who are "already embedded" in an institution that gives definition to a sermon.[14] Specificity about register at the micro level, however, involves understanding the detailed expectations of a particular location. Each preaching site is replete with its own collection of micro meanings determined by the expectations in that setting. For instance, congregants worshipping in Duke Chapel come with preconceived notions about what a sermon should be in a general sense, but they also carry notions about what a sermon in Duke Chapel should be—smart and clever. Their expectations help determine what they hear and will also influence what the preacher says because she, too, has preconceived notions about what people expect from a sermon in Duke Chapel. Because people expect to hear a "good" sermon in Duke Chapel, when they hear a bad one, they often fail to realize it, especially if it is delivered by one of the chapel's acclaimed pulpiteers. Here content receives definition, an expectation of "good," before the first word is uttered, but only as content is understood through relationship, since the assumption of those worshiping in Duke Chapel is that the preacher knows more than they do. So, while most of us who preach in this place agonize over the worthiness of our sermons, we could actually relax because people will assume that if the content is "bad" it must be because they failed to grasp something integral to its meaning.

Appreciating the difference between macro and micro registers helps illuminate the levels of meaning contained in each of the variables. In particular, at the macro level the context is merely the place where a sermon is delivered, most often a sanctuary during an organized worship service. At the micro level, however, place can have direct bearing on the meaning of a

---

14. Fish, "How to Recognize a Poem," 331.

woman as the preacher. Consider the following scenario: a woman delivers a sermon at two churches within a few miles of each other. The first sermon is preached in a university chapel to a crowd of mainline Protestants. She is neither the first nor the most renowned woman to stand before them. Later on the same day, she preaches at the city's largest Roman Catholic church to people who have come to celebrate a rite of passage for one of the church's members.

The context is different not only because the two churches are very different places but also because the content included in the gathering is different for the evening service. In spite of the fact that in both situations the preacher is the same and very little changes about how the parties communicate or even the relationship between them, the shifting context significantly alters the meaning of her words. The morning crowd arrived with the expectation of hearing a good sermon, while the evening crowd cared less about the quality of the sermon and much more about the person of the preacher. The people who had little or no experience with a woman in the preaching role, especially one vested with the symbols of authority reserved in their tradition exclusively for men, imparted greater significance to who was preaching than to what she said. The very fact that a woman was preaching in their sanctuary meant everything. Thus, for this event, the relationship dominates the meaning. The sermon preached that morning, however, allowed more space for congregants to glean meaning through the content and form of the sermon and for these variables to impart meaning to the whole.

Numerous examples might be provided to illuminate how the macro meaning of the sermon is filled with the micro meanings of each register variable. For instance, whereas one congregation might be excited about the novelty of a woman preaching, another with the same limited exposure to women as preachers might greet the same woman with apprehension. Here again the relationship dominates, but instead of anticipation leading to almost blind approval of the sermon, apprehension leads to nearly unanimous disregard for the sermon. In both instances, the place imposes a relational expectation, a sort of pretext for the sermon, that overshadows the entire communicative process, but in the latter example the congregation's relationship with the preacher impedes the meaning-making possibilities for the sermon. This is not to say that in either situation the meaning of the sermon is a foregone conclusion, but it is to recognize that the words spoken are freighted with meaning apart from their etymological existence.

Feminine Registers

Each of the register variables is useful for homiletics since the sermon derives so much of its meaning beyond the words spoken by the preacher. Altering a variable alters the homiletical possibilities and calls into question the reliability of the communication. If the culture constructs women as weak, irrational, and deviant (a common assumption at various stages of history), then the content of her speech will be overlaid with these perceptions. Thus, when she steps into the pulpit it is easier to rule her presence invalid and her words false, even if she utters the same words as a male counterpart.

Conversely, because of the ecclesial authority granted to the pulpit, a woman might gain a certain degree of respect through the act of standing before the congregation, even before she begins to speak. As Elizabeth Lawless points out in *Handmaidens of the Lord: Pentecostal Women Preachers and Traditional Religion*, women can get away with saying some things from the pulpit that they would never dare utter at home.[15] The importance of the relationship recedes in the worship space and the imbalance is moderated by what is happening at that moment. Since the relationship is about both who is speaking and who is listening, we see how multiple layers are at work in the reception of communication. In this register shift, discontinuity occurs between the discursive position (the pulpit) and the actual position (woman), subverting the official channels of authority and creating a new semiotic possibility.

The mode of communication further compounds all of these meaning-making possibilities, especially as they are manifest through the engendered body of the preacher. To begin with, the expected form of a sermon is generally declarative and authoritative, less often inquisitive or bemusing. Even sermons that end with a question usually assume the answer. The congregation that has been paying attention to the preacher for the previous fifteen minutes can readily answer the question, "What is God telling us through this story?" Suppose, however, a preacher sings his sermon, a form not often encountered in homiletics, although a few preachers are brave enough to sing a few bars of a song somewhere along the way. This delivery method would dominate such an experience and the other register variables would assume supporting roles in relation to it. In less extreme situations, how the sermon is delivered still has the potential to dominate the meaning-making possibilities.

---

15. Lawless, *Handmaidens of the Lord*, 167ff.

How the communication happens involves far more than whether the sermon is spoken or sung, shouted or whispered. It also involves how the speaker represents the words. Are the words offered earnestly or seductively, seriously or frivolously? A frivolous or seductive style could produce a register shift by diluting the integrity of the content—insincerity will not communicate authenticity—or altering the relationship—humor does not promote trust. Furthermore, within the tenor variable, the shift could be slight or extreme depending on the relationship between the communicating parties. If the relationship were fraught with suspicion, a seductive mode would cause little change because the congregation did not trust the preacher in the first place. If, however, the relationship is built upon respect and admiration, a seductive mode could erode the relationship by compromising the content and subject subsequent communication between the parties to misunderstanding through a variety of relational possibilities.

By acknowledging the engendered body of the preacher, we can explore other variable shifts that will affect the meaning of the sermon. Ruth Pidwell has demonstrated in a small sampling of preachers and their congregations the stereotypical perceptions projected upon the bodies of preachers.[16] She concludes that such projections can be attributed in large measure to the androcentric nature of the church. In her survey, Pidwell discovered that congregants who claim to focus on the undifferentiated "one in Christ" in the pulpit do not focus on gendered rhetorical distinctions. Congregants who do recognize and name the sexuality of the preacher read the preaching event through stereotypical gender lenses. She concludes that the cultural (I would add theological) script that congregants bring to the preaching event determines whether the sermon will be heard as gendered communication. Individual preachers can reinforce or challenge these determinants based on their own theological and cultural expectations of what it means to be male or female and the ways they enact these gender roles.

For instance, until recently only men could claim ecclesial authority, and so vestments for ecclesial leadership were typically considered men's clothing—long, flowing pulpit robes notwithstanding. When women (re)entered the ranks of clergy some fifty years ago, they dressed in these same robes and albs. Currently, Pidwell reports, women more so than men continue to vest when preaching rather than wear "street clothes." Women choose to wear "neutral" ecclesial clothing over their "gendered" feminine

---

16. Pidwell, "Word Made Flesh," 177.

clothing, but the fact that the neutral clothing, traditionally worn by men, actually looks feminine bends their identification back around again.

By dressing according to the standards of institutional authority, a woman manages to cloak the gender difference that her feminine clothing brings to the attention of the congregation. She subsumes her bodily difference under the garb of masculine power. Of course, this example offers the reminder that while men can present themselves as preachers from the pulpit—with or without ecclesial clothing—it is more difficult for women to present themselves as preachers without claiming the visual symbols of their professional roles. Furthermore, as Pidwell points out, the ecclesial clothing allows a female preacher to avoid being typecast into one of the negative tropes conventionally accorded to women by the church. A young, single, "sexy" woman, for example, can minimize the congregation's tendency to project onto her Eve-like images of temptation, passion, and chaos by wearing the symbol of the sacred and claiming for herself a "masculine" subject position that exudes power and authority.

In spite of numerous possibilities, the register shifts produced during a communication event are not limitless. In the examples cited above, for instance, context is crucial at the macro level, primarily because of the association of authority with the pulpit. Outside an ecclesial setting, however, the pulpit has little meaning-making potential. Though hard to imagine, consider bringing a hundred people who have never set foot in a church—or been indoctrinated by its protocol—into a sanctuary to hear a sermon. For these people, granting a woman access to the pulpit will carry no more weight than allowing her to stand on a tree stump in the yard (though many a tree stump has served well as a makeshift pulpit). The point is that the pulpit derives its status from a situational context that constructs and recognizes the pulpit as a place from which the church expects to hear people who know what they are talking about. The one hundred people outside of this context would not make this assumption, nor would they be able to determine if the preacher does indeed know what she is talking about because they would have no idea what she is talking about.

Of course, what this illustrates is that within an ecclesial setting, context at the macro level can supply almost unfettered acceptance. Authoritative place, coupled with the proper credentials for the one preaching, leads to a prediction about what will be communicated. For starters, we expect it to be "true." When something questionable is uttered it may take us a little longer to recognize it because it does not fall within the parameters of our expectations. Like the students who could not recognize another class's reading assignment because they were anticipating a poem, congregations may not recognize invalid claims from the pulpit because they are anticipating a truth from God. Examples abound: the exclusion of women, the enslavement of blacks, the ostracization of homosexuals. At the same time, because our conception of sermons suggests that we should pay attention to them, they can also work to challenge our preconceived notions by positing ideas that are marginal within society. Examples abound: the inclusion of women, freedom for blacks, acceptance of homosexuals.

Such contradictory claims are possible when the context dominates because those for whom Christian worship is a habit are not conditioned to enter the sanctuary suspiciously. Of course, biblical interpretation has direct bearing on both what is proclaimed from the pulpit and what is heard in the pews, again because of the many possibilities that are present through content and context. A "Lady Preacher," whether she acquires this title through merit or method, inherits centuries of authority granted to those who would preach, lacquered by interpretative strategies designed to deny her that authority. Those interpretative strategies can alter any of the communication variables and change the meaning of the sermon.

Changing Register to Change Meaning

The aforementioned authority involves far more than having something to say; it also requires being heard. Speaking is a fruitless endeavor until one is listened to and respected as a legitimate voice. Without this assurance the one speaking might expect to be excommunicated, if she is fortunate,[17] or burned at the stake, if she is not.[18] While the simple expectation that one will be heard without being harmed provides the impetus to speak in the first place, the matter is still more complicated. When the voice of the one speaking is considered inferior—"Can anything good come out of Nazareth?" (John 1:46)—those listening expect inferior words and have to be persuaded to pay attention in the first place. Voice is indeed connected to power, but those with the power to listen complete the other side of the coin. Tolerating the voice of another without truly listening only imposes silence through another means, and silencing the voice of another through

---

17. Florence, *Preaching as Testimony*, 17.
18. Malone, *Women and Christianity*, 2:207–19.

intimidation or punishment does not erase the communication; it redefines it through the relationship of the communicating parties.

Words spoken by someone bearing the insignia of inferiority, however, can go from meaningless to dangerous through their association with the one speaking. Consider the simple phrase "women should be allowed to vote." If spoken by a five-year-old seated at the dinner table in 1900, the words might be considered amusing or cute, at worst ill informed, but probably not devious. The words would be ignored because the one speaking is not old enough even to know what voting means. When spoken by a forty-year-old woman at the same table, however, the words go from cute to cunning. She creates resistance for the idea because she is deemed one who produces subversive, even dangerous, ideas. Listening accomplishes nothing because the words themselves are guilty by association; they have a negative effect rather than no effect.

A contrary imbalance is possible when the one speaking harbors disdain for those listening. In this case the communication is fraught with resentment, despondency, or contempt. The relational dynamic in such a scenario works determinatively with how the speaker communicates. Listeners will then evaluate the content in light of these other variables. Just as one expects she will be heard only after having been granted the authority to speak, one bothers to listen only after having been afforded respect by the speaker.

Within the relationship variable of the communicating parties, however, equality is less about sameness and more about balance. When one party in the communication dyad deems the other party inferior, the register shifts. Whether this shift occurs because those listening have no regard for the one speaking or the one speaking has no respect for those who are listening, the imbalance affects how they communicate and distorts the content of the communication. There is no simple formula for equality, however, and many theorists can demonstrate how equality works against the best interests of women. Equality through erasing the differences in style or appearance between men and women—putting all preachers in a black pulpit gown or a white alb cinctured at the waist—can produce androgynous pulpiteers cloaking the distinctiveness of a woman's proclamation in androcentric interpretations. Equality by homogenizing the illustrations and allusions within a sermon (no more sports metaphors or cooking illustrations) leads to generic sermons with which no one can identify. Neither alternative is a productive conduit for the wonder and mystery of God's word.

Balance or mutual respect between the communicating parties only touches the surface of the multiple nuances that produce meaning. Rebecca Chopp's work in education practices provides a portal for exploring register shifts that occur when word and deed are incongruent, creating imbalance in the field variable. According to Chopp, most education practices operate by transmitting ideas through ordered learning.[19] Foundational courses provide introductory material, which are followed by advanced courses offering greater mastery of a subject. The goal of this educational method is to reduce the gap between ideas and their application. Little thought is given, however, to how these ideas are practiced and lived out by those teaching or learning them, as if content could exist in isolation from the context that gives it meaning.

Consider the idea that women are called by God to preach. Most Protestant judicatories have embraced this idea for half a century. Meanwhile, the Protestant university chapel with which I am affiliated was led by straight white men for its entire history until the 2012 academic year, when for the first time a person of color became the University Minister. Still, a man. Hence, generations of undergraduate students have heard that women are called by God to preach, but the only evidence to support this idea is an occasional guest preacher, who necessarily comes bearing the designation "special." While special can have positive connotations, it also means not ordinary. Students are told that women preachers are ordinary and acceptable, but they see no evidence of it in this particular college crucible, and no student to pass through these hallowed halls has ever known a woman as the University Minister. On what basis should the students, whether male or female, believe the idea that women are called by God to preach?

Chopp suggests that we think of education as a process rather than a product and recognize that traditions gain their power through bodily enactment even as the tradition shapes our understanding of these bodies. The specific location of gendered bodies shapes our expectations about those bodies. Bodily enactment, therefore, provides the locus for change. When a woman occupies the pulpit, a place still conventionally considered the domain of men, the communication relationship lists to one side. As mentioned above, the pulpit as a place bearing expectations for truthtelling can override this imbalance, granting the speaker credibility by virtue of this place. Here a semblance of balance is restored, at least for

---

19. Chopp, "Educational Process," 111.

this particular communicative event, but because the practices in which we engage are generally guided by the norms we have come to expect, the woman will be listened to because she is in the pulpit and not because she is a woman.

Bringing equilibrium to the relationship requires changing our conventional notions about what it means to be a woman in leadership in the church. This will have as much, or more, to do with the subject matter informing our views of women and of God as it will with the women who are preaching. Since speech about God, inclusive of sermons, is education for the faith, it is likewise better conceived of as a process rather than a product. In this way, the necessity of naming God through a multiplicity of voices becomes more acute. Certainly, scripture and doctrine will inform ways to speak about God, but when these "products" are transmitted through a univocal proclamation they offer only a singular, and thus partial, representation. Even these somewhat rarefied products, canon and creed, can be enriched through a multiplicity of voices. Consider the biblical story that records the anointing of David by Samuel. While the story itself remains unchanged, it carries the potential for different images that will enrich the process of speaking about God. How would an older sibling imagine the anointing of a younger brother, especially if the older sibling is accustomed to receiving a "double portion"? How would a youngest child imagine this story, especially if the youngest child is already accustomed to getting "everything he wants," the lament of older siblings throughout the world? How would a mother imagine this story, especially given that David's mother is never mentioned, only his great-grandmother, Ruth? Imagining the story from the point of view of Samuel, who "tells" the story, may be the genesis of the imaginative process, but to make it the singular view is to curtail the process of experiencing God.

The very process of imagining the story invites a process of naming God, but the process is only as valid as the deference afforded the one who imagines it. When the imagined content is ignored because gender creates an imbalance, the imagination process is thwarted. Understanding how and why this happens can provide tools for naming our limiting tendencies in order to open up possibilities for deeper and fuller expressions for naming God without reverting to tokenism or becoming defensive. Tokenism politely listens to different meaning-making possibilities without ever seriously considering them. Defensiveness rejects uncommon offerings by dismissing them as obscure, trivial, or erroneous. These are only two limiting tendencies that work against the imagination process.

Chopp suggests that our tendency to limit can be overcome through a "process of networking around our commonalities and our differences."[20] The process necessarily involves putting into practice the theoretical and epistemological issues named by our present situation. Thus, passing a resolution in 1956 that recognizes the full clergy rights of women is meaningless until their rights are put into practice, again and again and again, in small rural churches and large university chapels. Until that happens the relationship will always list to one side when a women enters the pulpit. The imbalance may be influenced by the novelty of her presence, thus vesting her words with more importance than they deserve. Or it may be dominated by disdain for her audacity, freighting her words with unfounded suspicion.

Reconfiguring our notions of knowledge and how knowledge is acquired can help balance the relationship. How we ask the question can make all the difference for the answer we uncover. When necessary information is limited to empirical evidence an entire realm of knowledge is ignored. Answering the question about knowledge sources by pointing to the inherited tradition ignores the basic configuration of the tradition. Nor can we focus solely on the failure of the tradition to live into its own faith claims. It is too simple to claim that the experiences of women should now take priority over the revelation of God previously made known through scripture and tradition. One cannot replace the other. Instead, we should recognize that the revelation of God made known through scripture and tradition is itself a particular kind of experience preserved through the canon and creeds of the church. Other experiences are embedded in these dominant narratives of canon and creed. Exposing these contributory meanings does not threaten or discredit our knowledge of God but can deepen and expand it. Admitting that the journey to these codified convictions was more circuitous than the end result might imply should prompt us to be more generous toward the possibilities of our current journey and more open to the insight that comes from places seldom considered a source of knowledge.

It is also the case that some experiences from which knowledge might be gleaned have not been preserved at all. Acknowledging this reality should make us humble. While we cannot recover what history has failed to record, the awareness of privileged historical renditions should make us

---

20. Chopp, "Cultivating Theological Scholarship," 89.

Feminine Registers

more critical toward current communication tendencies. Loud and long voices dominant the places from which we receive information, but it could in fact be the case that the deepest truths about God come from the places of silence. Certainly, Elijah thought so (1 Kgs 19:12).

Knowing something about how listeners make meaning of the preaching event based on preconceived expectations within each register variable helps us understand how assumptions and cultural constructions often overwhelm the meaning of a sermon. At the same time communication occurs because of our common assumptions—with nothing in common we would stop listening. What we share, Fish's pretext, provides the basis for communication, but it also offers the place to amend what we know. When a woman preaches, her presence can produce new expectations by challenging old assumptions. New and different expectations introduce new possibilities for hearing God's word and responding to God's grace. When a woman steps into the "space between our meaning and our proclaiming," the word is born again.

5

Listening for the Register

Register provides an effective way to expose some of our preconceived notions about sermons, particularly when the preacher is a woman. As demonstrated previously, register involves a constellation of meanings through which the text comes to life at the intersection of three primary variables, most easily understood as content, relationship, and mode. Within each register variable the potential for meaning is governed by particular appropriations based on the relationship of the variables to one another in the communication event. As the variables change, register shifts occur that allow for new possibilities in communication, whether these meanings are assigned consciously or unconsciously by the communicating parties.

The following examples will show how a variable shift within the register allows preachers to create different meaning-making possibilities in their preaching. By appropriating different register variables, the preaching of women can both disrupt and interrupt expectations about the meanings in a sermon in ways that enrich the proclamation of the gospel.

The most obvious starting point for understanding variable shifts is with content and context, not because they are the most important but because they are so obvious. By adding the strands of women's experiences to sermon construction, we begin to revise the conventional language, images, and metaphors used in sermons. Women have knowledge of different aspects of life than do men, but their knowledge has not always been considered necessary or normative. Modifying what counts as valid knowledge allows us to include different sermon content and thus expand the ways we come to know God. This will lead, in turn, to new ways of articulating the gospel message. While such a shift privileges sermon content, the ramifications will extend through the relationship between the preacher and the congregation along with the form of communication used in the sermon in ways that cast new meanings on old ideas.

Christine Smith

Borrowing the weaving metaphor from Christine Smith, we can liken preaching to a piece of fabric.[1] The warp strands, representing norming traditions, are first placed on the loom lengthwise, and then the weft strands, representing women's experiences, are passed back and forth through these lengthwise strands to create the patterns of the fabric. To change the impression made by a piece of woven fabric, one simply turns the fabric over to the other side, thus foregrounding the weft strands. The complementary content remains present in the sermon, but the weft-faced preaching foregrounds the liberating possibilities available to women when they draw more readily upon their own experiences. Such preaching does not abandon the warp strands of the tradition—in fact, these threads are integral to the final product—but neither does it shy away from acknowledging those places where the experiences of women are in tension with some parts of the tradition. The location of the preacher as she or he constructs the sermon, on the warp side or the weft side of the fabric, will influence the meaning of the sermon.

The variable shifts through both content—intentionally including the experiences of women—and context—intentionally recognizing the standpoint of women. Such a variable shift is possible by redefining the function of authority in preaching, which then establishes different relational possibilities for the preacher and the congregation. Authority now comes from within the community rather than over it, modifying the interpersonal dynamic between the preacher and the congregation. Such a move does not imply that sermon construction is a democratic process, but only that the oligarchy of the pulpit encounters some checks and balances along the way.

Unless preachers confront preconceived notions of authority replete with their attendant biases, they will find it hard to change the content of the sermon. The subject matter of sermons will continue to reflect the same expectations and experiences of authority that have rendered the experiences of women insignificant for those who preach sermons and those who

1. Smith, *Weaving the Sermon*, 59ff.

hear them. Only when the relationship between the preacher and the congregation is modified can the preacher offer different content and privilege different contexts. The woman preaching and the congregation listening to her must believe that her voice matters before the content of her sermon will ever be heard.

When preachers privilege the social context as a fundamental building block for sermon construction, they create the possibility for new meanings. Locating the genesis of the sermon process in relational experience provides space to deconstruct the values of the dominant meaning-making systems influencing conventional biblical interpretation and congregational traditions. These dominant systems do not disappear, but they become subordinate to the experiences of the particular context. Scholars have repeatedly shown how the dominant systems dictating our conventional understandings of text and tradition also arose within their own contextual surroundings—surroundings that rarely included the contextual experiences of women.[2] Such recognition reveals the truth that the norming tradition is no more "objective" about scriptural meanings and theological interpretations than the subjective, relational experiences preachers privilege in sermon construction. All interpretation is relational and contextual. Knowing something about where she stands in relation to the congregation is part of the hermeneutical commitment for the preacher. Understanding how her relationship to the congregation is constructed through the social dynamics of a specific place influenced by years of traditionalist meaning is also integral to the meaning-making possibilities of her sermon.

Recognizing how the relationship between the preacher and the congregation influences sermon content helps illuminate the importance of how the sermon is proclaimed. For example, it is not enough to preach about sin and evil—content variables—if our sermons do not lead us to change the sinful situations, especially as sinful situations are determined in relationships where we seek to love God and neighbor. A relationship of hierarchy, found in most conventional preaching, is antithetical to the collaboration necessary for resisting evil as a systemic force in our world. To begin with, sin and evil are merely generic concepts until we personally encounter them and can name their specific impact on our lives.

Smith believes weeping is the requisite first move in resisting "radical evil."[3] Confronted by the reality of sin and our complicity in systemic evil,

---

2. See Ruether, *Sexism and God-Talk*, 12ff.

3. Smith defines radical evil as an "interlocking mass of oppression . . . that goes to the very roots of our common life" ("Preaching in Response," 18).

we can do no other but weep. Weeping embodies confession. This confession is not simply a ritual of personal piety nestled within an hour of worship—content that might have very little effect on our relationships. Instead, measured against God's holiness, confession is the only honest response to the world around us. It is truth-telling that incites us to active resistance, not simply in defense of ourselves, but as a purposeful response utilizing our resources and our activities to resist evil. Smith's model is helpful for articulating how the relational aspects of preaching determine meaning-making possibilities for the content and delivery of a sermon. When we can "weep and passionately feel," a relational characteristic, we will be moved to "confess the truth of the oppressions," content specific, and be propelled to "evoke resistance and action,"[4] a particular method of communicating.

Resistance and action call us to stand in places where we can struggle against evil. To illustrate this point, in one of her sermons Smith tells the story of two social workers who spend their days assisting women on the streets of Los Angeles, where there is a high risk of contracting AIDS. During a meal that Smith and some of her seminary colleagues shared with the social workers at the end of the day, the discussion turned to the moral implications of their mission. In the face of academicians who wanted to debate virtue, the social workers replied, "AIDS is not a moral issue, it is a health issue." Smith then says in her sermon,

> There is a vast difference between participating in academic discussions and distributing outreach bags of condoms and bleach. Transformational work is not about remaining still and defending ourselves against the evil that surrounds us, but it is a movement into it, and through it, with speech and presence and action. It is about gathering up our outreach bags with whatever it takes to get the job done. It is work that places our lives in fundamentally new places, sometimes positioning our passions and our bodies in dark and cold corridors that feel like death.[5]

Smith's point is that the world of these women who are at high risk for getting AIDS is not magically transformed by the social workers who seek them out and offer them tools to resist AIDS. Their world is the same, but the inevitability of their lives is resisted. The work of resistance offers the possibility of a different future for these women. They do not have to die of AIDS. The work of transformation goes on in the faithful acts of resistance

---

4. Smith, *Risking the Terror*, 13ff.
5. Ibid., 27–28.

in which we engage, even as the reality of transformation awaits God's consummating future. Content and relationship dictate action.

For Smith's project to succeed, she must necessarily deconstruct some conventional christological assumptions. Conventional understandings of sin, for example, typically reflect male experiences: for Augustine, pride; for Luther, willfulness; for Edwards, overindulgence; for Barth, disobedience. On the other hand, "negation of the self"[6] has been identified as particular to the sinfulness of women. Thus, for women, sin is not manifest through pride, willfulness, overindulgence, or disobedience, but rather through the internalization of blame and guilt. An appropriate response to this definition of sin, therefore, is not to repent of pride and willfulness, but rather to take pride in one's willful engagement of resistance. Considering the contextual situation expands the categories for sin and provides the means for a more authentic response. Thus, sin is not defined as either pride or humiliation; sin is defined by the situation that produces pride-filled or humiliating events. The description of sin in relation to the defining characteristics elicits the action for the communicative event.

The definition of sin takes on additional meaning when Smith directs our attention away from conventional assumptions of authority as understood by the communicating parties. For Smith, a change in the relationship is revealed in her Christology. Like some other feminist scholars, Smith resonates with the life and teaching of Jesus but protests the obsession over Jesus' passion and death. She suggests that "Jesus' ministry has revelatory power for us today, but it cannot have exclusive and ultimate authority."[7] In other words, the activity of the historical Jesus enables us to grasp the power of incarnation in our lives today. This concept owes much to feminist theologian Rita Nakashima Brock, who maintains that the saving event of Christianity must be larger than Jesus and his relationship to God, but inclusive of Christ within the community of which Jesus of Nazareth is a historical part.[8] For Smith, the point of the gospel is not that Jesus is in sole possession of power but that a new definition of power is now possible through the community, the body of Christ. With a new definition of power comes a new definition of the relationship between the communicating parties. Jesus' authority is not suffocating for adherents of Christianity, but liberating in its solidarity with them.

6. Saiving, "Human Situation," 25ff.
7. Smith, *Weaving the Sermon*, 88
8. See especially Brock, *Journeys by Heart*.

Feminine Registers

The death of Jesus, then, is not essential but tragic. It is not salvific because it satisfies a soteriological equation, but because the community responded creatively to the tragedy. Jesus' death testifies to the powers of oppression because it results from suffering inflicted by others and does not arise from the natural flow of life and death. Pointing to Jesus in order to claim that all humans suffer ignores this important distinction. Smith insists that by entering the places of systemic suffering we recognize such suffering is not inevitable and those who suffer can never be reduced to the status of victim. Daily survival joins with daily resistance, imparting a sense of agency to those who suffer. In preaching on the scene from the Gospel of Mark in which Jesus cleanses the temple, Smith offers this interpretation:

> Jesus has been drinking so much pain, has wept so many tears, has been close to so many who hurt. . . . He is not outraged at a few isolated, exploiting merchants, nor is he most concerned with the spiritual nature of God's house. He is anguished over an entire system that oppresses the masses while the social and religious elite prosper. . . . He has come to a moment when weeping is not enough. He places his body in direct resistance to the powers that exploit. . . . Will a few overturned tables and scattered coins bring the seat of power down and transform the lives of the poor? Maybe . . .[9]

How the preacher articulates the location of Jesus in relation to the congregation will be influenced by where the preacher stands in relationship to their own suffering. The preacher might stand with the congregation in the midst of suffering or instead stand near them, at a safe distance from the real pain. Changing this variable can change the dynamics of the relationship as the preacher proclaims a vision of the reign of God now made tangible by concrete experiences of resurrection and not through private salvation expectations.

Smith emphasizes oppression in much of her work, a category that blends elements of the context and relationship since the subject of oppression cannot be understood apart from the relational dynamics that produce it. For Smith the cross embodies the place of suffering and offers a valid portrayal of the lives of women. She does not, of course, claim that women have a monopoly on suffering—the physically and mentally handicapped receive a great deal of attention in her work—but believes that because suffering has a prominent place in the lives of so many women, it necessarily

---

9. Smith, *Risking the Terror*, 60–61.

informs their meaning-making potential. Within this setting, relationship is almost always comprised of unequal conversation partners: oppressor/oppressed, perpetrator/victim, strong/weak. Smith insists the "minor" voice is actually the legitimate voice in this dyad, and it is the task of preaching to champion those voices that have been silent for so long or that remain silent because their speech has been taken from them. The preacher is the voice of the voiceless, subverting the expectations of relational authority in a world that habitually privileges the voices of the majority. The relationship to suffering informs the response. The response to suffering defines the relationship. The sequence is not important because the register variables are interdependent.

Just as Weeks insists we must identify the standpoint out of which transforming action emerges, Smith is calling us to move into the places where resistance is needed and become active agents of resistance. Resistance preaching must first make an honest assessment of the present world and offer the invitation to construct a different world. The idea of resistance preaching surely can be traced back to Jesus, many of whose sermons offered tactics of resistance to those who were listening.[10] The ones listening to such sermons are invited to understand the oppression being addressed in these stories of resistance to the point that we "weep and passionately feel" them ourselves and then move into the places where resistance occurs. One of Smith's sermons provides this description:

> This is no disembodied faith. Sometimes it is dramatic and public. It is the martyr's blood that rises again in the people of El Salvador. . . . It is the incarnated presence of English and Welsh women at Gresham Peace Encampment in England who pitched their lives around the perimeter of a missile base for years—not months, but years. . . . Sometimes embodied faith is quiet and private. It is there as lovers hold each other in hospital beds, as condoms are used intentionally and with care, as babies are nursed, as children are fed, as people find safety in each others' arms, as wounded people find within themselves the strength to forgive, as a hand is extended to a stranger. I believe that when these things happen in our common life, whenever and wherever people refuse to abandon life, we are standing in the presence of resurrection.[11]

Here Smith demonstrates how each of the register variables influences the communicative possibilities by pointing out the obvious: when power is

---

10. Resistance is the interpretation that Walter Wink gives to the famous statement "turn the other cheek." See *Powers That Be*, 99ff.

11. Smith, *Risking the Terror*, 116.

only about might and money, the possibilities for resurrection life are circumscribed by the powerful. Just as limiting definitions of power truncate the word of God, so do narrow gender constructions render invisible other expressions of our human relatedness. By recognizing and honestly assessing our assumptions and convictions, we change how systems of meaning are configured. In the sermon section above, Smith's catalogue of powerful places offers a different vision for empowering people of faith. Power is not found in the missile base housing weapons of mass destruction; it is located in the camp of women just outside the fence.

Preaching constructs a reality, but the site upon which one stands to weave the sermon cannot be universalized or generalized.[12] It must always be a matter of working together on redemptive and liberating possibilities in the particular situations in which we find ourselves. Our theological claims must be embodied practices, which will create new understandings of relational life. This kind of salvific activity allows people to move from oppressive situations to places of empowerment. By using resistance as the guiding principle, Smith illuminates the complexity of conventional theological interpretations, challenges conventional expectations about the relationship between the preacher and the congregation, and offers her gendered self as one called to proclaim the word. In so doing, Smith provides a homiletical model that allows women to flourish and enhances the proclamation of God's word.

Lucy Lind Hogan and Anna Carter Florence

Where Smith calls us to reimagine content by complicating our understanding of relationship and embodiment, the work of Lucy Lind Hogan and Anna Carter Florence illuminate the priority of relationship. Hogan's work reflects a willingness to accept the androcentric starting place of biblical and ecclesial tradition and then attempts to move toward a feminist awareness by looking for places within these structures that allow for the possibility of women's voices—a relationship from the inside. Florence challenges some of the conventional constructions, but in doing so offers substantive reconstructive possibilities—a relationship from the margins. Like Christine Smith, both of these scholars write as Protestants, comfortably located in traditions that have recognized women as clergy for several

---

12. Ibid., 6.

generations; Hogan is an Episcopal priest and Florence is a Presbyterian minister.

Preachers are theologians, Hogan reminds all would-be preachers.[13] She is certainly not the first to make this claim. Karl Barth regularly claimed that all theology is preparation for preaching. More recently, Richard Lischer early and often reminds students that "preaching is the final expression of theology."[14] Like them and others, Hogan grounds her preaching among the theologians, insisting that whether a preacher begins the task of sermon preparation by consulting the lectionary for the assigned texts or by considering the social and political climate affecting the lives of her parishioners, a theological foundation undergirds the sermon process. In other words, sermons begin with the preacher's theological reading regimen. Each preacher, perhaps unconsciously, engages in selective appropriation, interweaving of passages, and creative reconstruction related to that preacher's discursive position. This discursive position includes what the preacher has predetermined a particular text might have to say about the situation and the preacher's knowledge of the congregation for whom the sermon is being prepared. Sermon preparation is an interpretive task undertaken by the preacher on behalf of the congregation, the guidelines of which are established in the relationship between the communicating parties. How the preacher configures this relationship determines much about the communicative possibilities for the gospel.

Florence likewise privileges relational configurations in order to create space for women's voices, but defines these relationships from the "outside." She points out that historical prohibitions against women preaching forced them to reclassify their proclamation as testimony. Thus, while the past is ripe with the proclamations of women, the discipline of homiletics is bereft of their presence.[15] Using testimony as her prism, Florence problematizes the conventional definition of "preacher" in order to recognize the women who have faithfully proclaimed the gospel even when ecclesial structures excluded them.

Testimony, according to Florence, is "a narration of events and a confession of belief."[16] The one testifying must tell what was seen and heard

---

13. Hogan, *Graceful Speech*, 13.

14. Lischer, *Theology of Preaching*, 26, and the opening lecture of every "Introduction to Christian Preaching" class he teaches.

15. Florence, *Preaching as Testimony*, xix.

16. Ibid., xiii.

Feminine Registers

(from the biblical text and the present life) and then confess what she believes about it. What she claims cannot be proved to those around her, only believed or rejected by those listening. Testimony as a valid representation of sermons exposes the relational dynamics that relegate the words of women to the margins of proclamation. When preaching expands to include this category, then the words of women become part of the record even while their relational position places them outside the institutional structures.

For Hogan the relationship of the communicating parties occurs within a structure of mutual accountability legitimized through persuasive rhetoric; for Florence the one testifying intentionally remains outside the place of respectability, which then affords her the opportunity to be heard. Hogan shows us how women fit into the established preaching regimen in order to proclaim a different truth, but Florence demonstrates how difference from the margin challenges the truth of the center.

To understand the difference, consider the following two sermon excerpts. When describing Mary's reaction to Gabriel's announcement from the Gospel of Luke, Hogan preaches,

> Mary's response to this astounding epiphany is born of a faith that has been nurtured by her family and faith community. Even though a young teenager, she has cultivated a deep inner life with a wide openness to God's presence. She has contemplated the great commandment of her faith, "You shall love the Lord your God with all your heart, mind, soul, and strength." Mary's deep love for God has made her ready to respond to God's call. Recognizing that all of this is indeed of God, Mary offers herself as a willing participant in the wondrous workings of the Divine Lover.[17]

Hogan's description of Mary is safely within the boundary of conventional theology—Mary displays a communally nurtured faith, she reacts with trust, and she responds in willing submission. Hogan does laud her faith and courage, but Mary is not described as one who challenges the conventions established by centuries of interpretation.

Compare that interpretation to this excerpt from one of Florence's sermons. Florence tends to write specifically of women who challenge conventional expectations, often paying a high price for their behavior. In constructing this sermon on a reading from the book of Esther, she directs our attention not to Esther, but to Queen Vashti:

17. Hogan, "Preaching the Lesson," 28.

> Even though the atmosphere is as charged with testosterone as any you will ever find, Queen Vashti does not do as any obedient subject of the king ought to do when given a direct order. She does not shuck her clothes [and] swallow her pride. . . . Queen Vashti is probably the first woman on record to *just say no*. . . . The story spreads. . . . They find that Queen Vashti's example has let loose a tidal wave of rebellion among the women of the empire.[18]

Rather than focus on Esther's courage through the remainder of the sermon, Florence goes on to describe Vashti's defiance as the impetus for the choice Esther must make in order to save the Jewish people. It is not deep faith and abiding trust that propel Esther, but the "dangerous memory" of Vashti's challenge. Florence describes Esther as the one who "finishes what Vashti started." This description of Vashti qualifies for what Weeks has earlier called negation from the inside. Vashti refuses to participate in negative practices and thus begins to alter the reality for those trapped within such systems. Preaching from the margin offers the potential for change, even if the choices one makes are limited by the surrounding structures. Mary, on the other hand, as described by Hogan, finds places within the structure that offer her liberating possibilities and chooses to engage in those practices. How each homiletician decides to re-member the subject of her sermon is grounded in a particular relational system, but both strategies succeed by recognizing and modifying the relational possibilities of the respective situations.

The different methods used by a preacher to establish the communicating relationship within a sermon influence the preacher's choices about sermon content. Hogan not only describes the relational possibilities for the communicating partners within the sermon but also considers the reality that these partners are in conversation with the Holy Spirit, the biblical text (replete with a plurality of past and present interpretive voices), dominant personalities within the church and within the preacher's life, and the world beyond the doors of the sanctuary.[19] The multiplicity of voices provides rich possibilities for the sermon, especially when all the voices are deemed legitimate. Like Chopp, Hogan encourages us to embrace the differences, hearing from one another fragments of God's truth that we can integrate into our own theological systems. A willingness to embrace diversity allows us to include different material and new ideas in the sermon,

---

18. Florence, "Woman Who Just Said No," 38f.
19. Hogan, "*Homiletos*," 4.

a relationship shift that influences sermon content. Because one sermon is but one fragment, one contribution, to a larger conversation, a single sermon should never be expected to encapsulate the whole truth or to provide the only truth about God. The relationships within a specific place allow for certain ideas to take shape within that sermon, which then joins the multitude of other conversation fragments from the past and contributes to the conversation moving us into the future. The conversation fragments of each sermon unite with previous proclamations and await inclusion in future proclamations by drawing on the memory of earlier relationships and adding their voices to future possibilities.[20] Recognizing that conversation partners engage in and are surrounded by overlapping power dynamics, preachers must embrace the "holy conversation" that will strengthen and redefine our relationships to one another.

Because sermons are theological conversations, not only are the conversation partners a crucial piece of the proclamation, but the nuances of their respective conversations must be considered for the preacher to adopt an appropriate communication mode. To interpret this dynamic, the preacher must know something about the congregation's "perceptual screens."[21] Each person listens to the preacher through a perceptual screen, a "pair of glasses through which [one] sees the world." The perceptual screen influences how one hears the sermon. An important part of the screen is the faith of the individual listener and the faith practices of the community surrounding that listener. For centuries, if throughout history, women have been the majority of the listeners, while the message was crafted for a male audience or at best for a "neutral" audience coded as human but conceptualized as "man."[22] Obviously, the world beyond the doors of the sanctuary looks different for women than it does for men, particularly related to the gendered division of labor. While some women do hold such high-profile jobs as Supreme Court justice, university president, and chief medical officer, the vast majority of women continue to work in the lower-paid service fields related to child care and health care.[23] Furthermore, in spite of the fact that most women now hold a full-time job outside the home, the division

---

20. See also Lischer, *End of Words*, 45, who offers a nuance to Hogan's fragmentariness of preaching by suggesting that each week the preacher "represents to the world *another* world" by proclaiming "glimpses of redemption" that if seen in whole would surely kill us.

21. Hogan, *Graceful Speech*, 81.

22. Braude, "Women's History," 88.

23. Malos, "Politics of Household Labour in the 1990s."

of labor within the home has changed very little.[24] Added to the differences for men and women outside the sanctuary is the reality that the dominant personalities within the church are heard differently by men than they are by women, even when the voice originates from the same person.[25]

Such a dissonant mode forces women listening to the sermon to reinterpret the content in ways that make sense for their particular relational realities. Listeners have always made decisions about what they hear in the sermon based on these perceptual screens, but when gender becomes part of the acknowledged relational dynamic between the preacher and the congregation, the preacher can make different choices about sermon content. Content begins to reflect the lived lives of all the listeners, balancing the relationship and establishing a more authentic mode for the claims being made by the preacher.

Preaching, of course, is more than a conversation between equal partners. The preacher is the one recognized by the community as having been called by God, educated at an accredited seminary, and credentialed by an appropriate judicatory. This dynamic creates a power disparity during the sermon delivery. Hogan acknowledges this power differential and uses it to make a distinction between persuasive power and coercive power. Coercive measures, according to Hogan, allow no alternatives for those who are confronted by them. Persuasion, on the other hand, operates by providing alternatives for the listener and allowing the listener to make an informed decision. Naturally, the preacher hopes the listener will be persuaded in favor of the preacher's position, but the preacher should never coerce cooperation.[26] We agree because we are persuaded, not because we are forced.

Persuasion may not be that innocent, however. The level of authority vested in the one occupying the pulpit creates a power differential that is manifest at multiple levels. What the listeners hear is greatly influenced by the register defining the particular experience. Persuasion as "an invitation to change that is offered in an atmosphere of freedom and openness"[27] is

---

24. Hochschild, *The Second Shift*. Hochschild summarized more than a decade of research to show that in 80 percent of two-parent American families, women are responsible for the majority of household and child-rearing tasks regardless of their demographic circumstances.

25. Gilligan, *In a Different Voice*, 31ff.

26. The problem of reducing the gospel to a rhetorical tool such as persuasion raises another set of issues that have been previously addressed by Richard Lischer. See Lischer, "Why I Am Not Persuasive."

27. Hogan, "Rethinking Persuasion," 8.

an atmosphere that must be created by the preacher. The preacher, therefore, must be more cognizant of the multiple power dynamics influencing the register of the sermon than are the listeners. For instance, if one's understanding of the authority of Jesus is closely related to his being male, then ecclesial authority will likely be granted to men only and will have a particular effect on how the sermon is heard when a woman preaches. If one's concept of the authority of Jesus is closely tied to the words attributed to him by the gospel writers, then textual authority will likely be rigidly defined in those specific instances when Jesus was believed to be speaking, which will influence the sermon content. If one's concept of the authority of Jesus rests in the life and teachings recorded in scripture, then historical authority might be found in the witnesses who reflect those teachings, perhaps related to content, but with implications for how the sermon is heard as well. Each of these "perceptual screens" create meaning-making shifts that will influence how the congregants hear what the preacher is saying and will have a bearing on how "persuaded" they really are.

While Hogan directs her attention to creating space within the church for the voices of women, Florence starts with the premise that women are not equal conversation partners in the power grid of preaching. This power discrepancy has a direct bearing on Florence's understanding of how a sermon is heard. For Florence the mode of preaching is not persuasion but testimony. Though the one testifying may hope the listener is persuaded by what she has to say, confessing the truth about what one knows matters more than persuading the listener it is true.

To illustrate her claim, Florence uses the lives of three well-known female testifiers: Anne Marbury Hutchinson, Sarah Osborn, and Jarena Lee. Each of these women intentionally stood outside the power structures around them, testifying from the margins and staking a claim on God's truth from where they stood. They did not pursue recognition by the power centers in the form of ordination or ecclesial membership, but those places of power finally had to recognize them precisely because they did speak from the outside. The relationship of inequality set up the medium of testimony and affected the content of what the women said—all of which determined what their listeners heard.

By focusing on three very different women from distinct eras, Florence draws out some of the major themes of feminist theory as it relates to homiletics. Anne Hutchinson challenged accepted historical hierarchies by raising questions about an established order that subjugated women in colonial Boston.[28] Had Hutchinson challenged their authority by demanding acceptance into their circle of control, her story would have concluded with a simple rejection. Instead, she never sought their power and thus challenged the very systems—ecclesial, magisterial, and domestic—by which they claimed power for themselves.

A century later, the story of Sarah Osborn unfolds against the backdrop of revivalism in Newport, Rhode Island, with its intermingling of the traditional and the unconventional.[29] Using "providence" as the means to understand how God provides the material goods necessary for survival and the spiritual confidence required to move boldly into God's future, Osborn met the challenge of proclaiming the gospel to a constant parade of eager students—as many as five hundred a week. She wrote her own biblical commentaries and then expounded upon these texts, offering an interpretation of scripture from a woman's perspective.

Almost contemporaneous with Osborn, Jarena Lee, a free black woman living in Philadelphia, claimed her place in history by spending over thirty years as an itinerant preacher in the African Methodist Episcopal Church. Endorsed by Richard Allen, the denomination's founder, Lee rode the wave of the Second Great Awakening with her "unlearned" style of revivalist preaching.[30] Holding to the doctrine of sanctification—belief in one's holiness before God—Lee understood her call to preach as a choice between the Holy Spirit and church polity. She followed the Spirit.

Florence uses the lives of these women to explain how testimony accurately defines preaching because it focuses our attention on the "distinctively Christian way of *speaking* and *knowing* (which is to say, *interpreting*)."[31] For Florence, the mode of Christian speech is testimony, but testimony also includes biblical interpretation,[32] creating space for the testimony of women to be integrated into the power grid of preaching. The mode grants validity to the relationship, and once the relationship is deemed valid, the content of the speech can be duly considered. Anne Hutchinson's case proves the point. In order to discredit the content of her testimony, Boston Colony authorities attacked her relationship to the community. Hutchinson, they claimed, had violated the relationship by ignoring their directives; there-

---

28. Florence, *Preaching as Testimony*, 12ff.
29. Ibid., 23ff.
30. Ibid., 49ff.
31. Ibid., 64.
32. Ibid., 74ff.

Feminine Registers

fore, anything she said was illegitimate. Those who heard her testimony, however, heard truth, and this truth legitimated her relationship to them.

With testimony established as a mode of faithful communication, it becomes apparent how sex roles and power dynamics influence the event. One's experience can only be understood in light of one's place.[33] This place—or standpoint, to use a previous term—offers a perspective that can be shared with anyone willing to listen even when what is heard makes no sense. Testimony need not persuade. Preaching as testimony insists that preachers stand in their own lives rather than the lives they wish they had and focus on the biblical text rather than the text of the world. From the context of our lives and the text of scripture, the preacher offers a description and profession of faith.[34]

The importance of this concept for preaching as it relates to women draws on Chopp's definition of the "perfectly open sign."[35] Not only is the word of God a perfectly open sign, but the possibilities for hearing it are also open.[36] Certainly most of us would agree that Martin Luther King Jr.'s "I Have a Dream" speech, proclaimed on the Mall in Washington, DC, was more sermon than speech, and the Gettysburg Address delivered by Abraham Lincoln from the platform of a train was more homily than address. Each example is testimony and each testimony is proclamation. This definition makes it possible to legitimize the work and words of women who have "promoted the reign of God" for thousands of years and unleashes preaching from the confines of church sanctuaries and the parameters of an order of worship by broadening the definition of a sermon.

An expanded definition of the sermon directs our attention to the obvious truth that women "read and interpret the Bible differently from the men of their day."[37] This happens because women tell what they have seen and heard in the biblical text while standing within their own lives—lives different from those of the men around them. Consider this excerpt of a sermon by Florence, based on the second chapter of Exodus:

> But in baby Moses' case, there were three other people the Pharaoh didn't count on: the midwife, the mother of Moses, and the daughter of Pharaoh. They wouldn't play ball. The midwife feared

33. Ibid., 82ff.
34. Ibid., xxviii.
35. Chopp, *Power to Speak*, 31.
36. Florence, *Preaching as Testimony*, 95ff.
37. Ibid., xix.

God, the mother loved her baby, and the Pharaoh's own daughter had compassion on the abandoned child. They each had to break the law to save the life of that baby. That tells you a lot about them. And they weren't saints. They were ordinary people acting under extraordinary circumstances, whose faith, love, and compassion made them more than they were.[38]

These three women were, quite simply, standing in a different place than was Pharaoh. They were standing with the baby, not against him. They saw the baby, heard the baby, and held the baby. For Pharaoh, the baby was distant and, therefore, absent from his decision-making process. And that is the point: women as preachers must stand firm within their own lives and speak the truth—testify—as they know it from this place. It remains true whether Pharaoh believes it or not.

Hogan and Florence both demonstrate how different relational possibilities allow register shifts within preaching. Preachers working within the authoritative structures can craft sermons that create negation from the inside. By selecting practices that privilege value-creating alternatives, these sermons plant the seeds for a flourishing future. On the other hand, sermons standing in the margins suggest that preaching involves more than the conventional definitions offered by those in power. By expanding these relationships, the sermon makes room for God's "perfectly open sign." Each possibility creates new ways of hearing God's word by finding space for the words of women to become part of the proclamation of the gospel.

Mary Catherine Hilkert

Unlike the previous homileticians, Roman Catholic Mary Catherine Hilkert practices her art within an ecclesial structure that prohibits the ordination of women. While ordination is not synonymous with preaching and Hilkert does her share of preaching, it remains the case that women who preach in the Roman Catholic Church are "special." It is also true, at least at this point in history, that the 1983 *Code of Canon Law* reserves preaching the eucharistic homily to those who are ordained. Thus, Hilkert cannot preach at Mass. Her location in this particular tradition lends another perspective to the voices of women precisely because she does not assume those voices will be heard.

---

38. Florence, "At the River's Edge," 33.

Feminine Registers

Hilkert defines preaching as "the art of naming grace found in the depths of human experience."[39] Much contemporary preaching suffers from an overreliance on dialectical theology, emphasizing the transcendence of God against the sinfulness of humanity, and leaves us with a "law-gospel paradigm for preaching."[40] The "dialectical imagination" that has marked so much preaching emphasizes the distance between God and humanity by describing the hiddenness of God and the sinfulness of humanity. A theology of preaching based on "sacramental imagination," on the other hand, pays more attention to God's loving presence, the goodness of creation, the mystery of the incarnation, and the power of the Holy Spirit within the community of faith. Still, as a Roman Catholic, Hilkert must contend with the reality that the sacramental imagination she advocates is emerging from a tradition that denies sacramental authority to women.

Pointing to Jesus as the paradigm for all Christian proclamation, Hilkert notes that Jesus announced the reign of God not merely through his words, but more so through his person and his actions.[41] Preaching then, in the manner of Jesus, is both word and deed. Hilkert insists that preaching include

> all the activities in which the baptized promote the reign of God. ... Women in prison ministries, women caring for battered women and abused children, women providing shelter for the homeless, women keeping vigil at the bedsides of the sick and the dying, and women involved in legal advocacy or political lobbying on behalf of the poor ...[42]

Action is part of proclamation, so it includes not only what we say, but also what we do. While broadening the definition of preaching legitimizes the work of women that has "promoted the reign of God" for thousands of years, it does little to change the register of the sermons heard within worship as long as women are excluded from this setting. Hilkert addresses the need for this missing ingredient by describing two separate occasions when the parish priests made way for someone from the congregation to offer the homily. Having been present for each of these worship services, she concludes that

---

39. Hilkert, *Naming Grace*, 49.
40. Ibid., 14.
41. Ibid., 158.
42. Ibid.

in both cases it was not only the hearing of the word in a woman's voice or from an African-American perspective that moved the assembly, but also the embodiment of the word by that specific woman and by the African-American preacher. It is a bold claim to assert that limited and even sinful ministers of the word nevertheless, by the grace of God, incarnate the word; but that is indeed part of a truly incarnational theology of preaching.[43]

The proclamation offered by these particular individuals was not sensational because the congregation got to hear a woman or an African American preach, but because the congregation got to hear the word embodied by people whose interpretation of scripture differed as a result of having lived different lives. The woman brought her gendered and raced body with her, and the African-American male brought his skin color and gendered body with him. In both situations, the mode of the communication began to shift before either preacher uttered the first word. When they did speak, this shift created the possibility for new insights on the content of their sermons. The new insights did not negate previous interpretations; rather, they enhanced and deepened the ways the congregation experienced God's word in their lives by expanding the sacramental imagination of those present.

Still, because preaching the eucharistic homily is reserved only for the ordained, most Roman Catholics will not experience the gospel "enfleshed" by a woman. This lacuna is what led Hilkert to expand the category of preaching in order to include the voices of women. She grounds her argument in a call for preachers to listen to human experiences for "an echo of the gospel."[44] Again, though, generalizing preaching to include a host of activities more appropriately catalogued as Christian practices, or even simply humanitarian work, presents an interesting challenge to the call for women to preach. Why allow a woman to deliver a sermon from a pulpit when she can prepare meals for the local soup kitchen—vested in her apron?

To stave off such arguments, Hilkert offers three qualifying criteria for her open-ended characterization of proclamation.[45] First, the "experience to be named is human experience in its depth dimension." This is not to say that human experience is God's word, but rather that God's word is revealed in particular historical experiences. Next, it must be acknowledged,

---

43. Hilkert, "God's Work in Women's Words," 14.
44. Hilkert, *Naming Grace*, 52–53.
45. Ibid., 49.

in today's world most people experience God "in the face of, and in spite of, human suffering." In the midst of this suffering a resilience exists that can only be attributed to the "Spirit of God within humanity." Finally, the keys to identifying grace are "located in the biblical story and the basic symbols of the Christian tradition." These three criteria provide guidelines for sermon content, but the content receives credibility from the ones who identify with the experience. In other words, those listening must identify with the experience, which implies a relational congruence, or the content will have no meaning.

The word of God is embodied in each one whose experience falls within the three defining characteristics, even if few of us would pause to diagram grace in such an orderly way. Within these boundaries, Hilkert expands the criteria of whose experiences of grace are valid and the places where these experiences of grace may occur. Recognizing the signs for God in common locations is crucial to naming grace in the ordinary places of our lives. Naming grace in our ordinary lives allows for a transformed proclamation of the word and becomes a new mode of communication that endows the ordinary with the holy through our ability to hear a new truth.

Subscribing to this paradigm moves the preaching task from the dialectical emphasis on "the power of the proclaimed word to transform sinful humanity" to the sacramental activity of God in human experiences that effects a "real inner transformation of the human person."[46] Authority for proclamation now has less to do with adjudicated positions of power—ordination, consecration, etc.—and more to do with recognizing and declaring grace, a claim quite similar to the one made in the Gospel of Mary. Christian preaching should focus on Jesus as the Word of God disclosing both the mystery of human existence and the mystery of God, a relational emphasis that can be either accented or occluded by the sermon's mode. Accenting the sacramental requires telling the story of Jesus as a story of humanity united with God and understanding the incarnation as the mystery of God's word spoken within history. In this manner, all of creation is incorporated into the redemption made possible by the incarnation.[47]

Hilkert insists that in addition to naming the grace-filled experiences of our lives, preachers are also responsible for naming "dis-grace" in the places crying out for redemption.[48] Directing attention again to Jesus, she

---

46. Ibid., 46.
47. Ibid., 48ff.
48. Ibid., 111.

points out that Jesus willingly entered the places of dis-grace and ultimately suffered the dis-grace of crucifixion, reinforcing proclamation through embodiment. Naming dis-grace exposes it as antithetical to the will of God. In a sermon based on Isaiah 9, she explains,

> It sounds so beautiful—like a victory that was already achieved—until you realize that Isaiah spoke these words as a promise and encouragement to hold fast and to hope when Israel was facing one more foreign invasion; Assyria was at their door. Israel was facing military defeat and exile when Isaiah called for unyielding trust in a God who is "Immanuel," God-with-us. Isaiah announced what God would do in the future as if it had already happened. God's promise is that sure.[49]

The will of God is so grace-filled the preacher can claim hope for the future in the reality of the present. By redeeming Christ's death through resurrection, God shows dis-grace will not have the last word. Suffering is not necessary or expected but is sometimes a consequence of faithful living in a world that is antithetical to God's reign. In the face of suffering, the hope-filled content of the proclamation establishes new relational possibilities. Faithful living makes the promise of the resurrection real for our lives even in the midst of suffering.

Suffering witnesses to Christ's obedience to God's purposes, but the empty cross of resurrection manifests salvation and provides a legitimating reality for obedience. Suffering is not a necessary ingredient for salvation; it is the result of dis-grace in a world that continues "to wait with eager longing for the revealing of the children of God" (Rom 8:19). Meaning comes through hope in God, not through suffering. Jesus manifested this hope by means of his teaching, his actions, and his very being: life, death, and resurrection. He embodied grace in a way that influences the entire register through which the word of God is communicated. By refusing a one-dimensional interpretation of Jesus—a suffering body—and of the lives of women, preachers can transmit a different message about the value of women within the Christian faith. Messages from women may include suffering, but they also include acts of kindness, practices of hospitality, and advocacy work, all embodied through a different mode because they are performed by female bodies.

Sermons configured this way unite preaching with spirituality. Preachers are not only "bearers of the Word of God," as Karl Barth indicates, but

---

49. Hilkert, "Two Fingers," 84.

Feminine Registers

also "bearers of Wisdom." Discovering new language to describe the vocation of preaching helps shift our conventional understandings about who may be called to the task of proclamation. Some of the new language involves naming the fundamental roles for Wisdom personified in scripture: creating, saving, and guiding.[50] As bearers of wisdom, preachers use words to describe and actions to encourage a new world order reflecting the reign of God. In doing so, they participate in re-creative power. Prophetic words of truth and justice, echoing the "liberating lifestyle" of Jesus, coalesce around concrete appearances of God's reign whenever preachers become active partners in the work of salvation. By recognizing the relational possibilities inherent in our daily lives, preachers nurture the attributes that enable community with one another and, ultimately, "friendship with God."

The proclamation of word and wisdom does not flow from an empty, generic vessel. The preacher's body bears the word and wisdom by performing the acts of grace.[51] The preacher who inhabits this body has a specific role to play in the creating, saving, and guiding work of the Spirit within the community of faith. An explicit link between preaching bodies and proclaimed spirituality pushes us to acknowledge the ways our sexuality pervades all of our experiences, precisely because the presence of God's Spirit comes to us through our particular and specific experiences of history and community. If spirituality includes our bodies, our sexuality, and our politics, then the cultural and societal definitions of gender difference will influence how we bear the word and wisdom of God. How we bear the word and wisdom enriches the possibilities for creation, salvation, and relation with God.

Such thinking offers greater depth for the preaching task by expanding the locations where grace is named and hope is activated within the waiting world. Indeed, hope is activated in prisons, hospitals, and soup kitchens, but the deed cannot be separated from the word of grace. What Jesus did made sense because of what Jesus said. Otherwise, hanging around with lepers and prostitutes would be ridiculous. In order to locate the transforming possibilities of the word in the daily lives of ordinary people, such experiences must be named by the community of faith as manifestations of grace, or they will just as easily be categorized as triumphs of the human spirit. Acknowledging the places where women have traditionally performed grace-filled deeds moves preaching in the direction of recognizing

---

50. Hilkert, "Bearing Wisdom," 147ff.
51. Ibid., 143.

the silent majority occupying the pews every Sunday. Redirecting the focus of preaching from dialectical to incarnational will alter how the message of grace is communicated, which in turn will influence the meaning-making possibilities for all the recipients of the proclamation.

John McClure

A discussion of preaching models would be incomplete without considering poststructural analysis. Though not a self-proclaimed feminist scholar, John McClure's poststructural methods share the fertile ground where feminist theory has taken root in the arena of homiletics. Employing the tools of deconstruction, McClure unmasks the power dynamics inherent in preaching that have so often led to the exclusion and diminution of women's voices. Furthermore, a poststructural approach provides a critique of the gendered ways the church worships and the gendered ways we think about what we are doing when we worship, necessarily including the sermon. New language and different significations can be used to provide richer and fuller experiences of God's revelatory power in our lives.

McClure uses two primary tools to propose a workable homiletic in a postmodern age: deconstruction and othering.[52] Both of these techniques have been valuable to feminist scholars. McClure wants to "reorient preaching toward the 'other.'" He does this by deconstructing the four conventional authorities for preaching: scripture, tradition, experience, and reason. Uncovering our presumptions about preaching allows for an analysis of how these conventional authorities have colluded in rendering silent the experiences and voices of women.

The biblical text is the paramount decentering vehicle because of its power to de-position its hearers on behalf of others. Its very power is "centripetal," or other-directed, consistently decentering its readers by creating tension between their identification with the text and their identification with the culture.[53] Turning next to tradition, preachers must remember all those people the tradition has excluded and even harmed in order to appropriate a particular "memory." Because preaching necessarily makes use of memory as a means for navigating between the canon and the contemporary context, how memory is used will determine which traditions

---

52. McClure, *Other-Wise Preaching*, 7.
53. Ibid., 14ff.

are privileged.[54] Next, deconstructing experience quite simply requires us to dispense with the myth that there is a common, verifiable, and objective premise shared by all people. We can only welcome this truth when we overcome our fear of others by embracing their experiences of the Infinite.[55] Embracing others allows us to recognize the false dichotomy of fact-value. These concepts are not opposites on a pole, where faith has to be justified as feasible, but faith is more accurately expressed as "communicative reason."[56] Communicative reason recognizes that truth/knowledge occurs in the communication itself, inclusive of signifying categories like reference, representation, and symbolic disclosure. Beyond these signifying categories, however, one must acknowledge the discursive realities that determine how words are used by the communicating parties—a claim consistently demonstrated by register—which leads in turn to an appreciation for the different possibilities for proclamation when women preach.

This poststructural approach necessarily involves working from the margins. The margin, however, is not a place of weakness and self-deprecation on the periphery of power, but a place where readers and hearers meet to try to make sense of their contexts and the text.[57] By locating interpretation in the margins, different meaning-making possibilities will occur because the hegemony that typically rules at the center has less power. Those who exist on the margins have a view both of the power structures at the center and the cracks in those power structures. Those in the center typically see only their power, not the cracks in power and certainly not those inhabiting the margins. As the church finds itself less centralized in a postmodern world, the voices of those typically marginalized will become its greatest asset because of their unique view of the center. When their voices are taken seriously, those in the center, or those who previously considered themselves central, will gain additional insights about themselves. The relational categories of margin and center are integral to the communicative reason of collaborative preaching.

Collaborative preaching has four primary goals.[58] First, it helps the preacher overcome the narrowness of her own particular social location. Second, the readers and hearers not yet familiar with the biblical text are

---

54. Ibid., 28ff.
55. Ibid., 47ff.
56. Ibid., 97ff.
57. Sugirtharajah, *Voices from the Margin*, 2–3.
58. McClure, "Collaborative Preaching from the Margins," 37.

offered a means by which they can enter it without being made to feel inferior and illiterate. Third, collaborators are encouraged to reach beyond the doors of the church to welcome the stranger, who may actually be a close neighbor who never felt emboldened to cross the sanctuary threshold. And last, those who gather together in the margins form bonds of resistance to the dominant meaning-making systems around them and gain support from one another for living in a manner contrary to these systems. So, while the sermon remains a single-party communication event, it will represent a multi-party communication process.

Obviously, such a process is a long way from the pastor's study where, sequestered from the world, one sits down each week amidst commentaries, dictionaries, and lexicons to mine the scriptures in order to produce a sermon for Sunday morning. The preacher still brings her exegetical knowledge and preliminary theological themes to the collaborative process, but other members bring to the table their reactions to and questions about the text in an effort to discover the gospel in a way specific to this congregation. Such an exercise requires more than gathering perspectives from the Wednesday morning Bible study in order to prime the pump for sermon writing that afternoon; it requires a commitment on the part of the preacher to hear the voices of the community, all the voices, and make them a part of the sermon without imposing one's own "inductive impulses."[59]

Where and with whom the preacher stands will affect what she sees, but even when standing in the margins one should never assume complete identification with the others present. First and foremost, we must listen carefully to the experiences of others as they confront the biblical text within the context of their lives. Not to do so runs the risk of reducing the distinctiveness of another's encounter with the text into the sameness of our own. The empathic listening championed by Chopp is integral to this process. Without it the relationship remains unbalanced as the preacher retains complete control over what is considered valid for the sermon. Of course, the preacher will make value decisions throughout the sermon preparation process by guiding the discussion—not controlling it; by providing exegetical and historical information alongside the life experiences and wisdom provided by the other participants; and finally, by forming—weaving—the strands of the preparation process into a whole fabric for proclamation of God's word.

---

59. McClure, *Roundtable Pulpit*, 101.

Feminine Registers

In a world increasingly described as multicultural but habitually proscribed by immigration laws, a collaborative approach to homiletics provides a safeguard against reinscribing our own prejudices. How preachers use illustrations to correlate with specific ideas, image difficult theological concepts, and ground sermons in a relevant common experience often reinforces dominant norms.[60] Though sometimes an unconscious strategy on the part of the preacher, sermon illustrations both generate and legitimate a particular meaning-making system within a community of faith. Over time these impressions legitimate ideologies that may be dominant but are not universal and might not even be normative. The dominant ideologies employed by preachers in these illustrations can work against the preacher's own theological framework. For example, the repetition of certain competitive attributes—warriors and winners—coupled with specific valuations—victors and champions—gives a particular impression of what a Christian life should look like. Meanwhile, consistently referring to sports metaphors in a culture awash with record-breaking achievements and sports "icons" undermines some of the foundational claims of Christianity. We worship a savior who spends time with the outcasts—losers—and refuses to fight when challenged—a quitter. Or so the culture would say.

Similar "culture-in-consciousness" tendencies run through illustrations that employ gender stereotypes, racial claims, and political assumptions. When preachers capitulate to either foundational truths or radical subjectivities, they discount manifestations of the Christian faith as they are known and practiced in particular places at particular times. They also discount large segments of the community's faith practitioners by normalizing and defining what is "appropriate" faithfulness. Because the preacher's perspective is circumscribed by our own discursive realities, preachers must not allow ourselves to be delimited by what we have known and experienced in our own lives. The knowledge and experience of those who form our congregations can be invaluable to a right and true proclamation of the word.

Reading the Bible with others is a small undertaking in comparison to the work needed to deconstruct the tradition, experience, and reason that often predetermine the way we hear scripture. How we read the Bible is overlaid with each of these components as they are in turn overlaid with biblical interpretation. Imagine, for example, reading the story of Solomon's "wisdom" (1 Kgs 3:16–28) with a woman from the congregation mired in

---

60. McClure, "Other Side of Sermon Illustration," 2.

Listening for the Register

a custody battle for her children. Imagine reading the story against the backdrop of the infamous Baby M case of the late 1980s.[61] Imagine reading it with Mary Beth Whitehead... Such collaborative undertakings can produce unpredictable and unanticipated results, much like the unpredictable and unanticipated news heard in the gospel message.

---

61. In this case surrogate mother Mary Beth Whitehead, having carried to term and birthed a baby for whom Bill Stern supplied the sperm, decided to return the money Mr. Stern had paid her as a surrogate and keep the baby. The case became a national cause célèbre.

6

A New Register

All preaching becomes more legitimate with the "re-imagining" Chopp has already named as crucial to our public discourse. Putting equal numbers of women in equal numbers of pulpits is not the magic formula, though having more women preaching on a regular basis in more churches would be a strong start. The formula for right and true preaching is as distinctive as the locations in which God's word is manifest to the community of faith. Attention to places of grace, voices of truth, and expressions of love move all our proclamations toward the reconciliation promised in 2 Cor 5:19:

> God was in Christ reconciling the world to himself, not counting their trespasses against them, and has entrusted to us the message of reconciliation.[1]

Such reconciliation comes to us as a pre-existing gift, providing the example through which we begin to effect reconciliation in our own lives. If our proclamation is to reflect the truth of God's reconciling love, it behooves us to craft sermons that claim the reality of this reconciliation. As Richard Lischer writes in *The End of Words*, the most distinctive feature of the message of reconciliation entrusted to us as God's people and to those of us called to proclaim this word is "its willingness to risk itself by embracing others."[2]

1. Cited by Lischer, this verse provides the grounding for his own theological claims in *End of Words*.

2. Ibid., 134.

A New Register

Preachers attune to signs of reconciliation will necessarily be those who embrace others in an effort to cultivate compassion, achieve solidarity, and realize transformation. When these attributes make it into our sermons, gender differences are not made invisible but are highlighted as integral to the very message of reconciliation we hope to achieve. The differences we celebrate are not polarizing valuations, but examples of the rich diversity of God's creative power. No one sermon or single homiletical form will capture all the possibilities for God's reconciling gift in our lives. Every sermon and every homiletical style should point us toward this gift and lift up for us the possibility of reconciliation with God, with each other, and within ourselves. "Let it be with [us] according to your word" (Luke 1:38).

What, then, shall we say about women as preachers? At a very fundamental level, the acceptance and regular inclusion of women preachers is consistent with the gospel we proclaim: humanity is created in the image of God, God is incarnate in the person of Jesus, and the power of the Holy Spirit makes this creating and incarnate God present in each proclamation of the word. The voices of women preachers will do much to reframe our understanding of ourselves by helping us become accustomed to the wholeness of God's image in each of us and the integration of our whole selves into the proclamation of the word.

The fact remains, however, that preaching is a gendered cultural form and its conventionally conceived gender is masculine. Susan Durber points this out in her article "A Pulpit Princess? Preaching Like a Woman" simply by the title.[3] A Pulpit Prince, she reminds us, conjures up images of authority and charisma; a Pulpit Princess sounds "frivolous." Is it preaching or preachers who are so engendered, however? Preaching must not languish under a gender monolith simply because men have been preaching longer than women and without the opposition women have faced for most of the church's history. Pride of place makes preaching a man's world, but not without the eruption of women's voices through the fissures of history. To claim it does is to close the sign that is God's word summoning us into the future that is God's reign. Far better is to affirm the gendered cultural form of preaching and utilize gender inclusiveness to move toward a deeper understanding of this reign.

The preceding chapters have demonstrated this salient truth: sermons are different when women preach, and these differences arise because each of the register variables—field, tenor, and mode—shifts in particular

---

3. Durber, "Pulpit Princess?" 167ff.

ways. Within the field variable, the axis of gender identifies the location of women, the standpoint from which women produce meanings and are produced by them. Obviously, where the preacher stands dictates a great deal about what the preacher sees and consequently determines much about how the preacher articulates this perspective to others. New ways of seeing offer new possibilities for hearing. Tenor—the register component that defines the relationship between the communicating parties—dictates many of our expectations about who should preach. Furthermore, gender categories have produced relationships that define women in particular ways and assign to them particular roles. By recognizing new narrative identities, the dominant relational expectations can be reshaped to allow different interpretations to emerge and new relationships to form. Finally, gendered bodies provide a particular mode through which the sermon is heard. A gendered hearing celebrates the distinctiveness of our bodies and the particularities of the communication offered by them. Acknowledging the gendered particularities of our perspectives, the relationships defining us, and the ways we communicate provides the impetus toward what we can be and where we can go to enact alternatives to the existing order. The voices of women bring distinctive meaning-making possibilities to each register variable, which, in turn, offer transformative possibilities for hearing God's word.

Making Difference Matter

Such claims might appear self-evident in the mainline church since women now occupy all ecclesial levels, from local pastor to bishop; direct denominational boards and agencies; and teach in the seminaries and church-affiliated colleges. Yet, nearly 25 percent of young people from the mainline churches enter college without ever having heard a woman preach.[4] Meanwhile, if all the biblical heroes regularly invoked by the preacher are men, all the pronouns used in liturgy to reference God are masculine, and all the imagery consistently employed to portray God is androcentric, then the message for women is, at best, silence and, at worst, negation, while the message for men remains static. Introducing a feminine pronoun or a gynocentric image for special occasions only exacerbates the problem by

---

4. Florence, *Preaching as Testimony*, xxiv. This statistic appears to be slightly lower in the Methodist tradition, in which the appointment process places women in churches rather than relying on the churches to "hire" them.

reinforcing that these are not normal representations of God and, therefore, women are not regular participants in the image of God.

Because women were historically marginalized from the ritual practices and decision-making centers of the church, the register of communication within and about the church became increasingly androcentric. Theological claims and scriptural interpretations were shaped through this perspective, which, though not erroneous, gradually became exclusive, a process Farley explains in his discussion of the middle axioms.[5] Quite simply, if the people discussing scripture and disseminating information all share the same proclivities, they are likely to reach the same conclusions. After a while these conclusions become normative, not only for the people who arrived at them but for everyone else as well. When McClure offers the model of a "roundtable pulpit," he is admitting that Farley is right. More and different voices create a deeper appreciation of God's presence in our lives and a richer testimony of God's power in our world.

The consistent presence of women in leadership and the regular use of female imagery in our liturgy can begin to change our attitudes about what is definitive in the life of the church and for the proclamation of God's word. The voices of women bring their interpretations of canon and creed formed through their own experience and participation in these interpretive systems. Recognizing experience and participation as part of our theological heritage offers the opportunity to augment some of the ecclesiological structures that are built upon them. This kind of ideology critique, as McClure points out, involves discovering and uncovering the power dynamics that dictate our claims so we can see them and ourselves more clearly. Deconstruction need not imply destruction. In fact, it should lead to more authentic reconstructions of God's presence among us.

Additionally, the conflation of space with identity can send gendered signals into the congregation, influencing what we think we know. Some new architecture in some places softens the conventional aesthetic of preaching, but for many congregations the pulpit still conjures up the image described by Herman Melville in *Moby Dick*:

> What could be more full of meaning?—for the pulpit is ever this earth's foremost part; all the rest comes in its rear; the pulpit leads the world. From thence it is the storm of God's quick wrath is first descried, and the bow must bear the earliest brunt. From thence it is the God of breezes fair or foul is first invoked for favorable

---

5. Farley, *Ecclesial Reflection*, 40ff.

winds. Yes, the world's a ship on its passage out, and not a voyage complete; and the pulpit is its prow.[6]

In many churches the pulpit might as well be accessed by Father Mapple's rope ladder. As Virginia Purvis-Smith reminds us, more than six hundred years of Western Christian culture permeate our sanctuary designs, prescribing places and roles for the participants in the drama of worship. Congregants sit "down" in the sanctuary; preachers are lifted up in pulpits. Congregants passively receive God's word; preachers authoritatively mediate the sacred. In this configuration, the sanctuary architecture smothers new models of preaching, whether or not one has read *Moby Dick*.

Relaxing the relationship between space and identity helps diminish the conventional expectations of the preaching event. When the identity of the preacher changes, the space itself begins to look different. Imagine, for example, what the pulpit looks like when occupied by a pregnant woman preaching on the annunciation. When the space begins to look different, the proclamation begins to take on new definitions. Difference provides the enrichment possible through the transformational power of the word of God.

When identity goes to a deeper level than physical space, to the production of knowledge, faith, and ecclesiology, the culture of the church and the expectations from the pulpit begin to change. The experiences and the voices that have been silent, in this case the voices of women, join the public proclamation to produce a new future inclusive of their truth. This is nothing less than the transformative possibility of which Weeks writes and the transcendent future to which Chopp points. The transcendent future becomes the present reality when we embrace the "open sign" that is God's presence in our midst. Since the production of our narrative identity is constantly being formed and re-formed by the stories of others who are part of the narrative, the inclusion of other forms of knowledge produces new ways of thinking.

The key ingredients for this emerging narrative identity, according to Chopp, are empathy, solidarity, and transcendence.[7] More than sympathetic listening, empathy requires identification with someone whose story is different from one's own in order to imagine what life is like for that other person. One's own experiences may help inform an understanding of

---

6. Melville, *Moby Dick*, 43f. The reference to Melville's "pulpit" comes from Purvis-Smith, "Gender and the Aesthetic of Preaching," 224.

7. Chopp, "Reimagining Public Discourse," 44ff.

the other, but they cannot be the sole basis for conceptualizing the other's life. The life circumstances of the other must be imagined as one's own by accepting the invitation to be re-formed by a new narrative identity.

Transforming our narrative identity requires more than hearing and understanding difference. We must also live in solidarity with and embrace difference, forsaking our penchant to assimilate others into the dominant narratives of our lives. The public "we" is no longer univocal but is a tapestry of different bodies and different voices without the goal of promoting sameness as the basis for interaction. The differences are celebrated as a network of overlapping spheres in which everyone participates in speaking the narrative identity into being. No one is subsumed by another because of difference, but instead is welcomed by the community as an enriching voice offering greater texture to the whole.

Understanding the other in an attempt to identify with a particular narrative identity and hearing the other as a means of enriching one's own narrative identity leads to transcendence. Transcendence includes more than a vivid imagination; it also summons us to put into practice what we are able to imagine through the faith claims we are called to pronounce. Unlike Christine Smith, whose category of resistance was intentionally devoid of transcendental language, Chopp insists transcendent living trusts in the future in spite of the future-denying present. As women preachers continue to participate in the formation of the preaching identity, the form can be transformed. In this transcendent space where we are able to glimpse other spaces and other ways of being in relationship with one another, we can begin to alter who we are and change who we will be.[8]

Future Possibilities

Preachers are in the business of "futuring," to borrow a phrase that Rebecca Chopp uses to describe education.[9] The preacher concerns herself with the present intersection of the biblical text and the congregation's context in order to move into God's future. Obviously, sermons contain more than information about the Bible and more than suggestions for the congregation to behave differently; sermons address those things that form the future for those of us who would live hopefully into God's reign.

---

8. Ibid., 47.
9. Chopp, "Beyond the Founding Fratricidal Conflict," 463.

Feminine Registers

Symbolic language is one of the primary avenues through which God's future is portrayed for us, and scripture is replete with such symbolic language—from the plumb line and ripe fruit of Amos to the mustard seed and costly pearl of Jesus. The symbols are not constructed through random chance, but have a living power of their own that is only partially expressed and never completely grasped. It is part of their power that symbols continuously move us to further thought and action without exhausting their viability.

As has been shown repeatedly, however, dominant groups set the standards that create the symbolic "norm." In this paradigm power is maintained by undermining the competence and limiting the power of others. Such a competitive, influence-resistant style is the norm for most of our interpersonal interactions, and a relational, collaborative approach is considered deficient or weak.[10] In the preaching enterprise, however, neither the preacher nor the congregation is at the center, but rather the relationship. Controlling the symbols by limiting their definitions will no longer be germane when there is no tug of war between the preacher and the congregation over symbolic representations.

In her work on public discourses, Chopp suggests a strategy for developing relational structures that are collaborative rather than competitive. She begins by claiming that the "public is an 'imagined community' based on the narrative of memory, inclusivity, and shared commonness."[11] Adjusting this for preaching, the sanctuary becomes "a space to which persons belong," and in this space they constitute a public by virtue of their possession of a shared narrative identity. The sermon is the discourse presented to this public, enabled by a particular relationship that exists between the one preaching and the ones listening. Because the narrative identity has been shaped by the prejudices of those who told the story and defined the symbols, the assumed narrative must be subjected to ideology critiques in order to construct new narrative identities based on experiences that heretofore have not been represented in the public discourse. Women bear this identity and live these experiences.

Initially, this re-membering is resisted by the narrative identity of the public because it seeks to displace a narrative that is familiar to everyone, even if detrimental to some. Potential progress does not insure a willingness to change, as demonstrated by the children of Abraham, who announced they would rather make bricks, even without straw, than embark

---

10. Gilligan, "Joining the Resistance," 501ff.
11. Chopp, "Reimagining Public Discourse," 35ff.

on a life-transforming journey into the unknown. New stories often meet new resistance, but simply telling the stories begins to offer new shape to the narrative identity of an imagined community. The new story contains elements that were both forgotten and denied, helping shape and reshape narrative identity. Who we are is identified through the inclusion of new voices that question who we thought we were and help reshape who we will be.

These new stories are not presented as "the rest of the story," as if the concluding scene had been previously omitted, but are a different memory of a story that has already been told to its conclusion. When the new voices begin to speak, they do more than add material to a twice-told tale. They tell the tale through a new medium; thus they change the register by altering the relationship. The tale now has a different meaning, even though it is the same story.[12] What had previously been considered private is now announced publicly; those who had previously been ignored are now encouraged to speak; and what had previously gone unquestioned is now scrutinized through the ethics of responsibility. Adding new content creates a new relationship.

Since access to the center as the place of power and influence typically is gained only by accepting the dominant narrative, new voices and new stories are essential for reimagining the identity of the public and transforming the dominant narrative. When the new voices speak and the new stories are told, meanings that were always part of the narrative come alive as part of the meaning-making of the narrative identity and, in turn, help transform the center. So, for example, I can no longer accept my family's presence on a particular plot of land as the rightful inheritors of a land grant from the king of England in the mid 1700s. It is that, but it is also the invasion of an empire that destroyed the lives of an indigenous population who displayed great reverence for the earth, respect for the sanctity of life, and generosity toward those who ultimately displaced them. The narrative identity of the center can never be the same again after this story is added to the history, even if I keep the land.

The goal is not to achieve a single unified narrative—one voice that represents all of us—but to recognize and celebrate the multiple narratives that are essential to the whole narrative identity. Here the possibility of living differently and changing the outcome of the story presents itself through transformed narrative identity. Truth about the past combines with hope for the future by cultivating compassion for those whose stories

---

12. Ibid., 38.

are now part of the recognized narrative identity. The choices are no longer limited to denying the other's story or assimilating the other into the dominant narrative. Now both stories, all stories, exist within one another and for one another.

Using the same category that Florence employed to thicken the definition of preaching, Chopp also labels her narrative re-telling "testimony." She suggests that besides telling the truth as we have experienced it, testimony further summons us to be responsible to those who have suffered at the expense of the hegemonic center. Testimony as a judicial device invites the narrator to tell her own story in her own words. As a theological device, however, testimony involves not only a recitation of what one has seen and heard but also a confessional claim about what it means.[13] For Chopp, testimony seeks to tell the truth by "pointing to the absolute through the conditions of the particular." In other words, an absolutist claim such as "God is love" is meaningless unless it is rooted in a narrative identity that enables me to interpret a grace-filled moment as God's love and not merely a stroke of good luck. Not only must the narrative include an understanding of God, "open" as that may be, but it must also provide a working definition of love as manifested by God. The testimony makes an absolute truth claim about the love of God grounded in a particular narrative.

Next, testimony involves the summons to "attend to the other in a responsible fashion." Such response involves measuring historical inequalities through the absolute claim of God's preeminent liberating work. By first knowing something about the particulars of God's love we can recognize the oppressive conditions that are antithetical to God's reign. Finally, testimony opens up the narrative identity to a "polyglot public discourse." This discourse involves more than integrating a few new sights and smells into the same old story or substituting a new ingredient for an old one. In order for diversity to achieve transformation, new sources of knowledge, new types of information, and new ways of listening must become part of the testimony. The monologue gives way to a heterogeneous space held together by the interconnectedness of each particular narrative even while the narratives themselves work to transform the definition of the space.

Thus, when a woman begins to preach, she need not mimic the pulpiteers around her in order to legitimate her voice. She can announce to the ecclesial public her own narrative springing from the truth of her own story and, by so doing, summon the gathered community to see the future

---

13. Ibid., 40ff.

by living its claims in the present. The transformed relationship between the communicating parties creates space for transforming the meaning-making possibilities of the sermon.

Different versus Better

As more women enter seminary and enroll in the introductory courses on preaching required by most of these seminaries, some interesting remarks are frequently made about their preaching auditions. Comments from those who evaluate them include the observation that in comparison to the men in the class, women more often produce the "best" sermons. Their sermons are considered better researched, better written, and better crafted. Better, however, could mean different. Perhaps we have become so familiar with the way men see and describe the world that hearing a different description strikes us as better. When women who come from a different place with different experiences are emboldened to bring forth their proclamations from these differences, it sounds "better" because it is fresh and new, not necessarily because they are better preachers. Even when the content changes very little, it can sound different coming from a woman because of the potential shifts in the tenor and mode variables.

Celebrating the distinctiveness women bring to the proclamation event allows us to find within this proclamation transformative possibilities for our relationship with God and with each other. Transcending beyond the familiar is not a supernatural or miraculous event; it happens in the concrete activities of our daily lives. Consider, for example, how the prophet Jeremiah practices transcendence through a real estate investment. With the Babylonian empire bearing down on the city of Jerusalem, Jeremiah buys a plot of land and painstakingly records the details of the transaction as if he or his descendants will actually live there. Through this simple business transaction the future becomes the present as Jeremiah lives into the promise: "Houses and fields and vineyards shall again be bought in this land" (Jer 32:15). The fact that Jeremiah likely died in Egypt without ever taking possession of his property has no bearing on this act of fidelity in accordance with God's promises. The characteristics of this hope-filled acquisition transcend the temporal events of owning a particular piece of property.[14] Hope based on God must necessarily find expression through particular historical circumstances even while the hope itself cannot de-

---

14. Clements, *Jeremiah*, 195.

Feminine Registers

rive from these circumstances. Jeremiah's purchase of land is a temporal exercise pointing beyond itself to a God-given, open-ended, hope-filled future. God's hope-filled future reveals itself in tangible acts of faith carried out in the concrete world of buying and selling, giving and receiving, living and dying. God's hope-filled future reveals itself in the proclamation of the word offered faithfully by those who know themselves as people living into the reign of God. In this way, we become what we practice.

Women as preachers, then, are not trapped between the poles of shedding their female identity when entering the masculine preaching site versus feminizing preaching by privileging "essentialist" characteristics of nurture and sensitivity. Such bifurcation only reinscribes the erroneous belief that gender is a fixed entity. In reality, gender identities are constantly being constructed and reconstructed by the practices in which we engage, even if it remains the case more often than not that a woman will bear the burden of proof, Hua Mulan not withstanding.[15]

Obviously, gender boundaries are still quite real in our cultural imagination. Witness the confusion of having a woman as a serious contender for the Democratic nominee for president of the United States in 2008. Reporters and commentators often could not decide whether to discuss her clothing or her speeches in the early days of the primary campaign. When they finally decided to concentrate a bit more on her speeches, they spent as much time analyzing how she spoke as they did what she said.[16] In spite of that, her presence in the campaign helps redefine the fixed boundaries of who might legitimately run for president of the United States and recasts

---

15. In Disney's animated story *Mulan*, loosely based on the legend of Hua Mulan from the fourth century, the hero enlists as her family's representative in China's war against the Huns and goes to great lengths in order *not* to prove she is a man. Those assumed to be men are seldom expected to prove it. Those claiming to be women have at various times in history been subjected to invasive physical exams and more recently to genetic testing. For example, genetic testing for female athletes competing in the Olympics, instituted in the 1960s and mandatory until 1999, has now been modified to "selective testing." "Beijing has set up a sex determination lab to test female Olympic athletes suspected to be males. Suspected athletes will be evaluated from their external appearances by experts and undergo blood tests to examine their sex hormones, genes and chromosomes for sex determination, according to Prof. Tian Qinjie of Peking Union Medical College Hospital" ("Beijing Sets up Sex Determination Lab," paras. 1 and 2).

16. After an interview in Portsmouth, New Hampshire, in early January 2008, commentators spent the better part of the week talking about the tears in Hillary Clinton's eyes with little attention given to what might have produced those tears and almost no mention of the hour's worth of detailed policy talk that preceded her "emotional moment."

some of the gendered space within those boundaries. Women preachers strike the same chords, challenging all of us to embrace new definitions about gender and about the places where we perform gender.

Here the specificity of the body extends beyond biological concreteness to include the historically and socially constructed referents. The body does not remain materially the same while cultural forces swirl around it, but is itself produced by these forces. The specificity of a body, therefore, must be understood within these contexts and not only in its biological concreteness. If the body is a medium through which both the text and the context are viewed, the body of the one proclaiming God's word is inscribed with meaning before she begins to speak. A female body, then, offers a different version of scripture and a different interpretation of that text by her mere presence.

Of course, the church's willingness to hear difference without dismissing it as insignificant and irrelevant is the necessary first step toward credibility. The different voices must be heard, not merely tolerated. Without this "hearing" the different experiences of women continue to languish in obscurity on the margins. Working from the margins is not a detriment in and of itself, as McClure has demonstrated, since the margin provides a critical perspective of the center. It remains the case, however, that unless those who occupy the normative positions of power are willing to hear marginalized voices, the center is denied the possibilities for its own enrichment.

Mary Wollstonecraft is only partly right. Men do have the power to allow women to preach because they still occupy most of the privileged places within our ecclesiological structures; but men do not have the power to transform the preaching paradigm. Power is less about control and dominion and more about the capacity to produce change. Those on the margins—in this case, women—bring the transformational potential with them and offer it to those in the center. When this happens, the production of meaning within the center can shift, taking with it all who are part of the preaching register. The result is not that women are better preachers than men but that preachers, men and women, will become better when different voices interface with one another, transforming our understanding of one another and of God.

Bibliography

Althusser, Louis. "Ideology and Ideological State Apparatuses (Notes toward an Investigation)." In *Lenin and Philosophy, and Other Essays*, translated by Ben Brewster, 1–60. New York: Monthly Review, 1971.
Aune, David E. *Prophecy in Early Christianity and the Ancient Mediterranean World*. Grand Rapids: Eerdmans, 1983.
Beauvoir, Simone de. *The Second Sex*. Translated and edited by H. M. Parshley. New York: Knopf, 1953.
"Beijing Sets Up Sex Determination Lab for Olympics." http://news.xinhuanet.com/english/2008-07/27/content_8781161.htm.
Berger, Teresa. "Contemporary Church and the Real Presence of Women: Of Liturgy, Labor, and Gendered Lives." *Yale Institute of Sacred Music Colloquium: Music, Worship, Arts* 1:1 (2004) 95–103.
———. *Women's Ways of Worship: Gender Analysis and Liturgy History*. Collegeville, MN: Liturgical, 1999.
Bowie, Fiona, and Oliver Davies, eds. *Hildegard of Bingen: Mystical Writings*. New York: Crossroad, 1990.
Bradshaw, Paul, et al. *The Apostolic Tradition: A Commentary*. Minneapolis: Fortress, 2002.
Braude, Ann. "Women's History *Is* American Religious History." In *Retelling U.S. Religious History*, edited by Thomas A. Tweed, 87–107. Berkeley: University of California Press, 1997.
Bremmer, Jan N. "Magic, Martyrdom and Women's Liberation in the Acts of Paul and Thecla." In *The Apocryphal Acts of Paul and Thecla*, edited by Jan N. Bremmer, 36–59. Kampen, The Netherlands: Kok Pharos, 1996.
Brock, Rita Nakashima. *Journeys by Heart: A Christology of Erotic Power*. New York: Crossroad, 1988.
Butler, Judith. *Bodies That Matter: On the Discursive Limits of Sex*. New York: Routledge, 1993.
———. *Gender Trouble: Feminism and the Subversion of Identity*. New York: Routledge, 1990.
Buttrick, David G. *Homiletic: Moves and Structures*. Philadelphia: Fortress, 1987.
Carroll, Jackson W. *Women of the Cloth: A New Opportunity for the Churches*. San Francisco: Harper & Row, 1983.
Chopp, Rebecca. "Beyond the Founding Fratricidal Conflict: A Tale of Three Cities." *Journal of the American Academy of Religion* 70.3 (2002) 461–74.
———. "Cultivating Theological Scholarship." *Theological Education* 32.1 (1995) 79–82.
———. "Educational Process, Feminist Practice." *The Christian Century* 112.4 (February 1–8, 2005) 111–15.

Bibliography

———. *The Power to Speak*. New York: Crossroad, 1991.

———. "Reimagining Public Discourse." *Journal of Theology for South Africa* 103.1 (1999) 33–48.

Clark, Elizabeth. "The Lady Vanishes: Dilemmas of a Feminist Historian." *Church History* 67.1 (1998) 1–31.

Clark, Elizabeth, and Diane Hatch. *The Golden Bough, the Oaken Cross: The Virgilian Cento of Faltonia Betitia Proba*. Chico, CA: Scholars, 1981.

Clements, R. E. *Jeremiah*. Atlanta: John Knox, 1988.

Craddock, Fred B. *As One Without Authority*. Enid, OK: Philips University Press, 1971.

———. *Overhearing the Gospel*. Nashville: Abingdon, 1978.

———. *Preaching*. Nashville: Abingdon, 1985.

———. "Preaching: An Appeal to Memory." In *What's the Matter with Preaching Today?*, edited by Mike Graves, 59–73. Louisville: Westminster John Knox, 2004.

Degler, Carl N. *At Odds: Women and the Family in America from the Revolution to the Present*. New York: Oxford University Press, 1980.

Del Mastro, M. L. *All the Women of the Bible*. Edison, NJ: Castle, 2004.

Dewey, Joanna. "From Oral Stories to Written Text." In *Women's Sacred Scriptures*, edited by Kwok Pui-Lan and Elisabeth Schüssler Fiorenza, 20–28. Concilium 3. London: SCM, 1998.

Dube, Musa W. *Postcolonial Feminist Interpretation of the Bible*. St. Louis: Chalice, 2000.

Durber, Susan. "A Pulpit Princess? Preaching Like a Woman." *Theology and Sexuality* 13.2 (2007) 167–74.

Edwards, O. C., Jr. "History of Preaching." In *Concise Encyclopedia of Preaching*, edited by Richard Lischer and William H. Willimon, 184–227. Louisville: Westminster John Knox, 1995.

Epp, Eldon Jay. *Junia: The First Woman Apostle*. Minneapolis: Fortress, 2005.

Faludi, Susan. "Carol Gilligan: Different Voices or Victorian Echoes?" In *Backlash: The Undeclared War against American Women*, 325–32. New York: Crown, 1991.

Farley, Edward. *Ecclesial Reflection: An Anatomy of Theological Method*. Philadelphia: Fortress, 1982.

Fausto-Sterling, Anne. *Sexing the Body: Gender Politics and the Construction of Sexuality*. New York: Basic Books, 2000.

Firestone, Shulamith. *The Dialectic of Sex: The Case for Feminist Revolution*. 1970. Reprint, New York: Farrar, Straus and Giroux, 2003.

Fish, Stanley. "How to Recognize a Poem When You See It." In *Is There a Text in This Class? The Authority of Interpretive Communities*, 322–37. Cambridge: Harvard University Press, 1980.

———. "Is There a Text in This Class?" In *Is There a Text in This Class? The Authority of Interpretive Communities*, 303–21. Cambridge: Harvard University Press, 1980.

Florence, Anna Carter. "At the River's Edge." In *Sacred Strands: Sermons by Minnesota Women*, edited by Barbara Mraz, 31–37. Rochester, MN: Lone Oak, 1991.

———. *Preaching as Testimony*. Louisville: Westminster John Knox, 2007.

———. "The Woman Who Just Said No." *Journal for Preachers* 22.1 (1998) 37–40.

Fredriksen, Paula. "Beyond the Body/Soul Dichotomy: Augustine on Paul against the Manichees and the Pelagians." *Recherches Augustiniennes* 23 (1988) 87–114.

Frow, John. *Marxism and Literary History*. Cambridge: Harvard University Press, 1986.

Gilligan, Carol. *In a Different Voice: Psychological Theory and Women's Development*. Cambridge: Harvard University Press, 1982.

———. "Joining the Resistance: Psychology, Politics, Girls, and Women." *Michigan Quarterly Review* 29 (1990) 501–36.
Grosz, Elizabeth. *Volatile Bodies: Toward a Corporal Feminism*. Bloomington: Indiana University Press, 1994.
Hall, David, ed. *The Antinomian Controversy, 1636–1638: A Documentary History*. 2nd ed. Durham: Duke University Press, 1990.
Halliday, M. A. K. *Language as Social Semiotic: The Social Interpretation of Language and Meaning*. Baltimore: University Park, 1978.
Haraway, Donna. "Situated Knowledges: The Science Question in Feminism and the Privilege of Partial Perspective." In *Simians, Cyborgs, and Women: The Reinvention of Nature*, 183–201. New York: Routledge, 1991.
Hartsock, Nancy. "The Feminist Standpoint: Developing the Ground for a Specifically Feminist Historical Materialism." In *Discovering Reality: Feminist Perspectives on Epistemology, Metaphysics, Methodology, and Philosophy of Science*, edited by Sandra Harding and Merrill Hintakka, 283–310. Dordrecht: Reidel, 1983.
Hilkert, Mary Catherine. "Bearing Wisdom: The Vocation of the Preacher." *Spirituality Today* 44.2 (1992) 143–60.
———. "God's Work in Women's Words." *America*, November 27, 1999, 14–18.
———. *Naming Grace: Preaching and the Sacramental Imagination*. New York: Continuum, 1997.
———. "Two Fingers Under the Door." In *Just Preaching: Prophetic Voices for Economic Justice*, edited by Andre Resner Jr., 83–85. St. Louis: Chalice, 2003.
Hochschild, Arlie Russell. *The Managed Heart: Commercialization of Human Feeling*. Berkeley: University of California Press, 2003.
———. *The Second Shift*. New York: Penguin, 2003.
Hogan, Lucy Lind. *Graceful Speech: An Invitation to Preaching*. Louisville: Westminster John Knox, 2006.
———. "*Homiletos*: The Never-Ending Holy Conversation." *Homiletic* 21.2 (1996) 1–10.
———. "Preaching the Lesson." *Lectionary Homiletics* 17 (2005) 11–12, 27–28.
———. "Rethinking Persuasion: Developing an Incarnational Theology of Preaching." *Homiletic* 24.2 (1996) 1–12.
Holdrege, Barbara A. "Beyond the Guild: Liberating Biblical Studies." In *African Americans and the Bible: Sacred Texts and Social Textures*, edited by Vincent L. Wimbush, 138–59. New York: Continuum, 2001.
Hultgren, Arland J. *The Parables of Jesus: A Commentary*. Grand Rapids: Eerdmans, 2000.
Ice, Martha Long. *Clergy Women and Their Worldviews: Calling for a New Age*. New York: Praeger, 1987.
Jensen, Anne. *God's Self-Confident Daughters: Early Christianity and the Liberation of Women*. Translated by O. C. Dean Jr. Louisville: Westminster John Knox, 1996.
Jones, Serene. *Feminist Theory and Christian Theology: Cartographies of Grace*. Minneapolis: Fortress, 2000.
Jordan, Judith V. "Toward Competence and Connection." In *The Complexity of Connection: Writings from the Stone Center's Jean Baker Miller Training Institute*, edited by Judith V. Jordan et al., 11–27. New York: Guilford, 2004.
———, ed. *Women's Growth in Diversity: More Writings from the Stone Center*. New York: Guilford, 1997.
Jordan, Judith V., et al. *Women's Growth in Connection: Writings from the Stone Center*. New York: Guilford, 1991.

Bibliography

Kastner, G. Ronald. "Introduction to Eudokia's 'Martyrdom of St. Cyprian.'" In *A Lost Tradition: Women Writers of the Early Church*, edited by Patricia Wilson-Kastner et al., 135–46. Washington, DC: University Press of America, 1981.

Kelsey, David H. *Proving Doctrine: The Uses of Scripture in Modern Theology*. Harrisburg, PA: Trinity, 1999.

Kienzle, Beverly Mayne, and Pamela J. Walker. *Women Preachers and Prophets through Two Millennia of Christianity*. Berkeley: University of California Press, 1998.

Kim, Eunjoo Mary. *Women Preaching: Theology and Practice through the Ages*. Cleveland: Pilgrim, 2004.

King, Karen. *The Gospel of Mary of Magdala*. Santa Rosa, CA: Polebridge, 2003.

———. "Prophetic Power and Women's Authority: The Case of the Gospel of Mary (Magdalene)." In *Women Preachers and Prophets through Two Millennia of Christianity*, edited by Beverly Mayne Kienzle and Pamela J. Walker, 21–41. Berkeley: University of California Press, 1998.

Lawless, Elaine J. *Handmaidens of the Lord: Pentecostal Women Preachers and Traditional Religion*. Philadelphia: University of Pennsylvania Press, 1988.

Lazzarato, Maurizio. "Immaterial Labor." In *Radical Thought in Italy: A Potential Politics*, edited by Paolo Vierno and Michael Hardt, 132–46. Minneapolis: University of Minnesota Press, 1996.

Lee, Peter A., et al. "Consensus Statement on Management of Intersex Disorders." *Pediatrics* 118.2 (2006) e488–e500.

Lehman, Edward C., Jr. "Women's Path into Ministry: Six Major Studies." *Pulpit and Pew: Research Reports* 1 (2002). http://pulpitandpew.org/sites/all/themes/pulpitandpew/files/Lehman.pdf.

Lesko, Jeneane. "League History." *The Official Website of the AAGPBL*. http://www.aagpbl.org/index.cfm/pages/league/12/league-history.

Lischer, Richard. *The End of Words: The Language of Reconciliation in a Culture of Violence*. Grand Rapids: Eerdmans, 2005.

———. *Theology of Preaching: The Dynamics of the Gospel*. Nashville: Abingdon, 1981. Revised, Durham: Labyrinth, 1992.

———. "Why I Am Not Persuasive." *Homiletic* 24.2 (1999) 13–16.

Long, Thomas G. *The Witness of Preaching*. 2nd ed. Louisville: Westminster John Knox, 2005.

Lorde, Audre. "The Master's Tools Will Never Dismantle the Master's House." In *Sister Outsider: Essays and Speeches*, 110–13. Trumansburg, NY: Crossing, 1984.

Lose, David J. *Confessing Jesus Christ: Preaching in a Postmodern World*. Grand Rapids: Eerdmans, 2003.

Macy, Gary. *The Hidden History of Women's Ordination: Female Clergy in the Medieval West*. New York: Oxford University Press, 2008.

Madigan, Kevin, and Carolyn Osiek. *Ordained Women in the Early Church: A Documentary History*. Baltimore: Johns Hopkins University Press, 2005.

Malone, Mary T. *Women and Christianity*. 3 vols. Maryknoll, NY: Orbis, 2000.

Malos, Ellen. "The Politics of Household Labour in the 1990s: Old Debates, New Contexts." In *The Politics of Housework*, edited by Ellen Malos, 206–17. Cheltenham, UK: New Clarion, 1995.

McClure, John. "Collaborative Preaching from the Margins." *Journal for Preachers* 19.4 (1996) 37–42.

———. "The Other Side of Sermon Illustration." *Journal for Preachers* 12.2 (1989) 2–4.

Bibliography

———. *Other-Wise Preaching: A Postmodern Ethic for Homiletics*. St. Louis: Chalice, 2001.

———. *The Roundtable Pulpit: Where Leadership and Preaching Meet*. Nashville: Abingdon, 1995.

McGee, Lee, with Thomas H. Troeger. *Wrestling with the Patriarchs: Retrieving Women's Voices in Preaching*. Nashville: Abingdon, 1996.

Melville, Herman. *Moby Dick*. Edited by Harrison Hayfor and Hershel Parker. New York: Norton, 1967.

Miller, Patricia Cox. *Women in Early Christianity*. Washington, DC: Catholic University of America Press, 2005.

Morgan, Robin. "Goodbye to All That (#2)." The Women's Media Center, February 2, 2008. http://www.womensmediacenter.com/feature/entry/goodbye-to-all-that-2.

Noren, Carol. *The Woman in the Pulpit*. Nashville: Abingdon, 1992.

Økland, Jorunn. *Women in Their Place: Paul and the Corinthian Discourse of Gender and Sanctuary Space*. New York: T. & T. Clark, 2004.

Osiek, Carolyn, and Margaret Y. MacDonald, with Janet H. Tulloch. *A Woman's Place: House Churches in Earliest Christianity*. Minneapolis: Fortress, 2006.

Pidwell, Ruth. "The Word Made Flesh: Gender and Embodiment in Contemporary Preaching." *Social Semiotics* 11.2 (2001) 177–92.

Portailié, Eugène. *A Guide to the Thought of Augustine*. Translated by Ralph J. Bastian. Chicago: Regnery, 1960.

Purvis-Smith, Virginia. "Gender and the Aesthetic of Preaching." In *A Reader on Preaching: Making Connections*, edited by David Day et al., 224–29. Burlington, VT: Ashgate, 2005.

Radar, Rosemary. "The Martyrdom of Perpetua: A Protest Account of Third-Century Christianity." In *A Lost Tradition: Women Writers of the Early Church*, edited by Patricia Wilson-Kastner et al., 1–18. Washington, DC: University Press of America, 1981.

Ruether, Rosemary Radford. *Sexism and God-Talk: Toward a Feminist Theology*. Boston: Beacon, 1993.

———. *Women and Redemption: A Theological History*. Minneapolis: Fortress, 1998.

Saiving, Valerie. "The Human Situation: A Feminine View." In *Womanspirit Rising: A Feminist Reader*, edited by Carol P. Christ and Judith Plaskow, 25–42. San Francisco: Harper & Row, 1979.

Salzinger, Leslie. *Genders in Production: Making Workers in Mexico's Global Factories*. Berkeley: University of California Press, 2003.

Sanders, Cheryl J. "The Woman as Preacher." In *A Reader on Preaching*, edited by David Day et al., 211–23. Burlington, VT: Ashgate, 2005.

Schüssler Fiorenza, Elisabeth. *In Memory of Her: A Feminist Theological Reconstruction of Christian Origins*. New York: Crossroad, 1983.

Shroyer, M. J. "Aquila and Priscilla." In vol. 1 of *The Interpreter's Dictionary of the Bible*, edited by George A. Buttrick et al. Nashville: Abingdon, 1962.

Smith, Christine. "Preaching in Response to Radical Evil." *Living Pulpit* 1.4 (1992) 18–19.

———. *Risking the Terror: Resurrection in this Life*. Cleveland: Pilgrim, 2001.

———. *Weaving the Sermon: Preaching in a Feminist Perspective*. Louisville: Westminster John Knox, 1989.

Sugirtharajah, R. S. *Voices from the Margin: Interpreting the Bible in the Third World*. Maryknoll, NY: Orbis, 1996.

Tanner, Kathryn. "Inventing Catholic Tradition." *Horizons* 29.2 (2002) 303–11.

Bibliography

Tisdale, Leonora Tubbs. *Preaching as Local Theology and Folk Art.* Minneapolis: Fortress, 1997.

Tjaden, Patricia, and Nancy Thoennes. "Full Report of the Prevalence, Incidence, and Consequences of Violence against Women." Washington, DC: National Institute of Justice and CDC, 2000. https://www.ncjrs.gov/pdffiles1/nij/183781.pdf.

Torjesen, Karen Jo. *When Women Were Priests: Women's Leadership in the Early Church and the Scandal of Their Subordination in the Rise of Christianity.* San Francisco: HarperSanFranciso, 1993.

United Methodist Book of Worship. Nashville: United Methodist Publishing House, 1992.

Weeks, Kathi. *Constituting Feminist Subjects.* Ithaca: Cornell University Press, 1998.

Wesley, John. *The Works of John Wesley.* Edited by Thomas Jackson. Vol. 12. Grand Rapids: Baker, 1978.

Wilson-Kastner, Patricia. "Introduction: The Pilgrimage of Egeria." In *A Lost Tradition: Women Writers of the Early Church,* edited by Patricia Wilson-Kastner et al., 71–81. Washington, DC: University Press of America, 1981.

Wink, Walter. *The Powers That Be.* New York: Doubleday, 1998.

Wire, Antoinette Clark. *The Corinthian Women Prophets: A Reconstruction through Paul's Rhetoric.* Minneapolis: Fortress, 1990.

Wollstonecraft, Mary. *A Vindication of the Rights of Women.* 1792. Reprint, Mineola, NY: Dover, 1996.

The Women's Kingdom. Directed by Xiaoli Zhou. 2005. http://www.pbs.org/frontlineworld/rough/2005/07/introduction_to.html.

Name and Subject Index

abortion, 43
abstinence, 11, 12, 43
Acts of Paul and Thecla, 4–5, 12–13
African Independent Churches, 39
African Methodist Episcopal Church, 109
agency, xv, 7, 12, 24, 46, 58, 69, 100
AIDS, 98
All American Girls' Professional Baseball League, 41
Allen, Richard, 109
Althusser, Louis, 23, 23n60, 65, 65n28
Andrew, 17–18
androcentric, xi, 27, 29, 34, 45–46, 62, 76, 87, 90, 102, 124–25
apostolic, 15, 19
   succession, 19
Apostolic Constitution, 16
Apostolic Tradition, 3, 3n5, 11
Augustine, 69–70, 99
authority, xi, xv, 2, 7, 11, 13, 16, 18–22, 24, 31–32, 35, 42, 54, 67, 86, 88–90, 96, 99, 107–9, 114, 123
   divine, 21
   ecclesial, 86–87, 108
   figure, 78
   historical, 108
   institutional, 88
   Jesus, 99, 108
   power and, 74, 88
   preaching, 32
   proper, 8
   pulpit, 32
   relational, 101
   sacramental, 11, 112
   symbol of, 8, 85
   textual, 108

Barth, Karl, 99, 103, 115
Berger, Teresa, ix, xvn7, 11n34
Bible, xv, 3, 39–40, 51, 76, 110, 119–20, 127
biblical studies, xv, 46
biology, 68
birth control, 43, 73
body, xiv, 31, 46, 67–74, 82, 100, 116, 133
   Christ, 99
   engendered, 86–87
   female, 133
   gendered, 68, 71, 113
   human, 72
   image, 64
   physical, xiv, 68, 73
   preacher, 71, 116
   raced, 113
   suffering, 115
   types, 73
   unspoiled, 12
born again, 77, 79, 94
Brock, Rita Nakashima, 99
Butler, Judith, xin2, 23n61, 57–58, 61n21, 72n34
Buttrick, David, 26, 29–32, 35–36

Canaanite woman, 39
canon/canonization, 3, 9, 14, 16, 21–22, 52, 76, 92–93, 111, 117, 125
capitalism, 56
celibacy/chastity/continence, 11–13, 15
Chopp, Rebecca, xv–xvi, 35–40, 42–43, 68, 75, 91, 93, 105, 110, 119, 122, 126–28, 130
Christ, 6, 8, 18, 32, 70, 87, 99, 115, 122
Christian/s, xv, 109
   community, 2, 7

141

Name and Subject Index

Christian/s (*continued*)
  consciousness, 32
  culture, 126
  early, 13
  faith, 5, 115, 120
  life, 120
  martyrs, 2
  message, 45
  movement, 14
  practices, 113
  preacher, 18
  preaching, xi, 3, 54, 114
  proclamation, 112
  speech, 109
  teaching, 41, 43
  tradition, 19, 45, 114
  witness, 19
  worship, 89
  year, 54
Christianity, 2–3, 5–6, 9–10, 13–14, 16, 21, 24, 57, 63, 69–70, 76, 99, 120
Christology/Christological, 99
Civil Rights Act, 57
class, xii, 6, 12, 38, 43, 56–57, 62, 81
clergy, 10, 14, 25n1, 26, 87, 93, 102
Clinton, Hillary, 132n16
Code of Canon Law, 111
colonialism, 39, 109
communicative reason, 118
community of faith, also faith community, 6, 26, 51–52, 74, 104, 112, 116, 120, 122
compassion, 20, 24, 111, 123, 129
confession, 20, 52–53, 98, 103, 130
congregation, xii–xiv, 7–9, 23–24, 26, 30–31, 33–34, 51–53, 55, 61, 64–66, 70–73, 75, 78, 84–89, 96–97, 100, 102–3, 106–7, 112–13, 119–20, 125, 127–28
constructivism/constructivist, 27, 38n24, 71–72
Corinthians, the, 8–9
Corinthian women, 8–9
covenant, 37, 44, 53
Craddock, Fred, 26–30, 34–36
Crosby, Sarah, 1, 24, 25

Daly, Mary, 71

daughter, 12, 20, 40, 110–11
David, 53, 92
de Beauvoir, Simone, 61n21, 72
deacon/deaconess, 7, 10–11, 16, 20
deconstruction, 117, 125
Didascalia Apostolorum, 3, 15
difference, xi, 5, 25, 27, 29, 33–34, 37–38, 45–46, 62–63, 68, 72, 83–84, 90, 93, 98, 104–5, 107, 123–24, 126–27, 131, 133
  biological, 71
  bodily, 88
  equality and, 64
  gender, 29, 49, 88, 116, 123
  margin, 104
  psychological, 35
  relational, 29, 63
  sexual, 72
  social, xi
  theological, 8
discursive, xiii, 32, 48, 50, 55, 65, 86, 103, 118, 120
division of labor, see labor
dual/dualistic/dualism, 31, 36–37, 46, 69–71
Dube, Musa, 39–40
Durber, Susan, 123

ecclesiology, 4, 35, 46, 126
empathic/empathy, 119, 126
Epp, Eldon Jay, 9
equality, 57, 61–64, 66, 81, 90
essentialism/essentialist, xi, 27, 38, 62, 71–73, 132
Esther, 104–5
Eucharist/Eucharistic, 2, 6, 14, 20, 111, 113
Eudokia, 4
Eusebius, 19–21
experience, 15, 23, 27–28, 30, 33, 37–38, 40–41, 43, 45, 64, 73, 84–86, 93, 96–97, 100, 107, 110, 114, 116–20, 125–26, 128
  authority, 96
  codified, 40
  common, 79, 120
  contextual, 97
  different, 73, 131, 133

Name and Subject Index

faith, 33, 40
  hermeneutical, 52
  historical, 41, 113
  human, 28–29, 38, 112–14
  life, 119
  listener's, 28
  lived, 28, 30
  male, 99
  masculine, 45
  prophetic, 9, 15
  relational, 97
  women, xiv, 59, 76, 93, 95–96

faith/faithful, 2, 4–7, 10, 21–22, 26, 33n14, 33–34, 40–41, 61, 73, 83, 92–93, 98, 101–6, 110–11, 115, 118, 120, 126–27, 132
Faltonia Proba, 4
family, 5, 12, 44, 82, 104, 129, 132n15
  biological, 81
  configurations, 36–37, 45, 81
  form, 36, 44
  income, 43
  influence, 8
  leave, 82
  model, 37
  nuclear, 36, 44
  patterns, 44
  systems, 8, 37
  unit, 37, 81
Farley, Edward, 21, 77, 125
female, 10, 41, 108
  agency, xv
  apostles, 20
  athletes, 132n15
  body, 115, 133
  clergy, 26
  deacon, 10, 15
  identity, 132
  imagery, 125
  male and, xii, 2, 16, 26, 69–70, 72–73, 87, 91
  preacher, xi, 27, 34, 71, 88
  prostitutes, 6
  sacredness, 13
  sexuality, 76
  student, 26
feminism, first wave of, 62

feminism, second wave of, 62
feminist, xii, xivn5, xv–xvi, 27–28, 31, 38–39, 45–46, 62, 76, 81, 99, 102, 117
  homiletic, xvi, xvii, 46
  theology, 27, 99
  theory, xi, xvi, 27, 30, 32, 35, 55, 71, 108, 117
Firestone, Shulamith, 81–82
Fish, Stanley, 53n9, 77–78, 80, 82, 94
Florence, Anna Carter, xvi, 102–5, 108–11, 130
Frow, John, xiiin4, 48
Fulkerson, Mary McClintock, ix

gender, xiin3, xii–xiii, xv, 28–31, 33–34, 38, 49–50, 57, 60–61, 70n33, 72, 75, 92, 107, 123, 132–33
  analysis, xi
  assignment, xii
  asymmetries, 46
  axis of, 124
  barrier, 41
  boundaries, 132
  categories, 66, 124
  constructions, 23, 29, 50, 59–61, 71–72, 83, 102
  differences, 29, 49, 88, 116, 123
  distinctions, 34
  expectations, 42, 57, 66
  hierarchies, 76
  inclusiveness, 123
  identity, 58–59, 66, 132
  ideology, xvii, 64
  issues, xiii
  lenses, 87
  neutrality, 70
  norms, 57
  orientation of, 31
  perceptions, 34
  performance, 58
  preferences, xv
  production of, 72
  roles, xi, xiii, 60, 65, 87
  script, 20
  stereotypes, xi, 71, 120
  stratification, 10
  studies, xii

Name and Subject Index

gender (*continued*)
   systems, 9
gendered, xiii, xiv, 34, 43, 45, 55–56, 60–63, 65–68, 70–71, 73, 87, 91, 102, 106, 113, 117, 123–25, 133
gender-neutral, 70
genetic testing, 132n15
Gilligan, Carol, 62–63, 68, 73
glossolalia, 7
God, xvi, 8–9, 30, 34, 40–41, 45–47, 51, 54, 63, 69–70, 73, 86, 89, 91–92, 94–95, 97, 99, 104, 106, 109, 111–12, 114–16, 122–25, 130–31, 133
   call, 43, 104, 107
   children of, 115
   creation, 37
   father, the, 66
   fear, 111
   future, 31, 99, 109, 127–28, 132
   grace, 54, 77, 94, 113
   hiddenness, 112
   holiness, 98
   image, 46, 123, 125
   incarnate, 40, 123
   kingdom of, 79
   knowledge of, 93
   love, 122, 130
   mystery, 114
   people, 32, 122
   persistence, 33
   power, 117, 123, 125
   presence, 7, 30, 35, 39–41, 47, 66, 77, 79, 104, 112, 116, 125–26
   promise, 14, 115, 131
   purposes, 115
   reconciling, 123
   reign, xiv, 6, 79, 100, 110, 112, 115–16, 123, 127, 130, 132
   revelation, 22, 46, 77, 93
   salvation, 6
   spirit, 79, 114
   transcendence, 112
   truth, 105, 108
   voice, 9
   will, 54, 115
   wisdom, 116

   word, xi–xiii, 2, 26, 30, 33, 36, 51–54, 90, 94, 102, 110–11, 113–15, 119, 122–26, 133
   work, 41, 130
gospel, 1–2, 10, 15, 17, 20, 24–26, 28, 34, 36, 45, 49, 55, 70, 74, 99, 103, 107n26, 109, 113, 119, 123
   law, 112
   message, 15, 96, 121
   narrative, 18
   proclamation of, 62, 95, 111
   story, 28
   writers, 13, 108
gospels, 6, 17
   Synoptic, 18
Gospel of John, 16, 18, 22, 79
Gospel of Luke, 33, 104
Gospel of Mark, 16n47, 100
Gospel of Mary, 16–19, 22, 114
Gospel of Matthew, 39
grace, 54, 70, 77, 94, 112–17, 122, 130

Halliday, M. A. K., xiiin4, 48–49, 51
hermeneutic/hermeneutical, xi, 31–32, 40, 52–53, 97
heterosexual, 36–37, 44n36
hierarchy/hierarchical, 8, 11, 16, 18–19, 23, 36–38, 46, 56, 76, 84, 97, 108
Hildegard of Bingen, 22–23
Hilkert, Mary Catherine, xvi, 111–14
Hogan, Lucy Lind, xvi, 102–5, 106n20, 107–8, 111
Holdrege, Barbara, 51
Holy Spirit, 7–9, 52, 105, 109, 112, 123
homiletics/homiletical, xi–xii, xv–xvii, 26–27, 29, 34, 46, 54, 66, 68, 86, 102–3, 105, 108, 117, 120, 123
homosexuals, 89
Hutchinson, Anne, 58, 108–9

immanence, 68
Immanuel, 115
inequality, 62, 66, 108
interpellate/interpellation, 23
Isaiah, 115

Jeremiah, 131–32

Name and Subject Index

Jesus, 3, 6, 16–19, 39–40, 79–80, 99, 108, 112, 114–16, 128
  apostles of, 20
  authority, 99, 108
  Christ, 70
  death of, 16, 99–100
  deeds, 6
  historical, 19, 99
  inner circle, 2, 15
  interpretation of, 39, 115
  ministry, 99
  mother of, 20
  passion, 99
  person of, 14, 123
  stories about, 13
  teachings, 6, 16–18, 99
  tradition, 16
  warning, 12
  words, 6
Junia, xvn8, 9–10, 21

Kelsey, David, 51n4
King, Karen, 9n25, 16n45, 17n48
King, Martin Luther, Jr., 110
knowledge, xvi, 14, 37, 40–41, 51, 56–57, 69, 78, 93, 95, 103, 118, 120
  conventional, 45
  exegetical, 119
  forms of, 126
  history, 14
  inherited, 45
  production of, 126
  situated, xiv
  sources of, 93, 130
  spiritual, 17

labor/labor, division of, 43, 45, 55–56, 63, 65–66, 79, 106–7
laity, 24, 26n1
language, xvi, 30–31, 35–37, 42, 73, 79, 116–17
  church, 8
  conventional, 95
  feminist theory, 30
  hierarchy of, 46
  operation, 50, 83
  symbolic, 128
  systems, 30, 68

transcendental, 127
use, 36
Lawless, Elizabeth, 86
lectionary, xv, 54, 103
Lee, Jarena, 108–9
Levi, 17–18
Life of Macrina, 4
Life of Melania, 4
Lischer, Richard, ix, 103, 106n20, 107n26, 122
liturgy, 15–16, 46, 124–25
Long, Thomas, 26, 32–36
Lorde, Audre, 36
Lose, David, 52
Luther, Martin, 99

male, xi–xii, 2, 6–7, 9–10, 13, 16, 21, 23, 26, 34, 41, 69–70, 72–73, 80–81, 86–87, 91, 106, 108, 132n15
  African-American, 113
  bodies, 35
  disciples, 17, 19
  experiences, 99
  heroes, 46
  preachers, 34
  privileged, 13
  straight, 73
  white, 73
  writers, 13
margin, xiv, 20, 66, 102, 104–5, 108, 111, 118–19, 133
marginal, 89
marginalized, 6, 11–12, 14, 16, 18, 23, 42, 118, 125, 133
marriage, 11–12, 36, 37n20, 44n36, 57, 80
Martyrdom of Perpetua and Felicitia, 4–5, 12–13
Mary of Magdala/Mary Magdalene, xvn9, 1, 17–19, 21
maternal, 81–82
McClure, John, xvi, 117, 125, 133
meaning-making, xii–xiii, xv–xvi, 30, 40, 47, 55, 66–68, 73, 76, 78, 82, 85–86, 88, 92, 95, 97, 101, 108, 117–20, 124, 129
midwives, 57
mind, xvi, 28, 54, 61, 68–69, 104

145

Name and Subject Index

Moby Dick, 125–26
Montanists. *See* New Prophecy
Mosou people, 80–82
mother/mothering, 12, 15, 20, 23, 40, 43–44, 65, 73, 80, 92, 110–11, 121n61, 126
Mulan, 132, 132n15

New Prophecy, 4, 9n26
Nicene Creed, 41
Nicodemus, 79–80
Nineteenth Amendment, 57

ordination, xvi, 16, 19, 20n52, 25, 26n1, 35, 108, 111, 114
Osborn, Sarah, 108–9

passion, 41, 68, 88, 98–99
Pastoral Epistles, 9
paternal, 80
patriarchy, 56, 76
Paul, 3–10, 6n18, 13, 15, 17–18, 20, 69–70, 70n33
persecution, 13, 20
Peter, 17–19
pew, xii–xiii, 1, 36, 67, 89, 117
Phoebe, 6n18, 10
Pidwell, Ruth, 87–88
postcolonial, 39
practice, 2, 9, 23, 26, 40–41, 43, 45, 50, 56–59, 92–93, 105, 111, 127, 132
  birthing, 79
  Christian, 113
  church, 77
  community, 41
  compulsory, 58–59
  ecclesial, 13, 45
  education, 46, 91
  embodied, 102
  exclusionary, 71
  faith, 106
  historical, 58
  homiletic, 29
  hospitality, 115
  laboring, 56, 66
  local, 3
  marriage, 37
  naming, 80
  negative, 105
  preaching, 38, 46
  ritual, 125
  sexual, 11, 44
  signifying, 58
  social, 50
  symbolizing, 65
  traditions and, 53
preaching, xi–xiii, xv–xvii, 1–3, 7, 10–11, 14–15, 19, 26n1, 26–27, 29, 31–32, 34, 36, 42, 46, 50, 52, 59–60, 62, 65, 67–70, 73, 75–77, 79, 82, 84–85, 87–88, 94–96, 98, 100–104, 107–14, 116–17, 122–23, 125–26, 128, 130–31, 133
  analysis of, xiii
  authority, 31–32, 96, 117
  Christian, xi, 3, 54, 114
  class, 34
  collaborative, 118
  conventional, 97
  courses, 131
  deductive, 27
  early church, 14
  eucharistic homily, 113
  focus of, 117
  function, 55
  gender analysis, xi
  gendered, 123
  guild, 26
  hermeneutics, 31–32
  identity, 127
  illegitimate, 1
  inductive, 27
  liturgical, 14
  masculine, 132
  margins, 105
  mode, 108
  models, 117, 126
  narrative, 26
  opportunities, 77
  practices, 38, 46
  regimen, 104
  register, xvi, 54, 60, 133
  resistance, 101
  revivalist, 109
  role, 16, 20, 85
  site, 59–60, 84

Name and Subject Index

space, 73
spirituality, 115
strategies, 49
students, 35
styles, xii
testimony, 110
theology of, 112–13
vocation, 116
weft-faced, 96
women, 35, 46, 48, 85, 92, 95, 97, 103, 122
pretext, 55, 82, 85, 94
prophets, 7, 9, 20, 131
prophetic, 7–9, 15, 19, 116
prophetess, 20
psychology, 63, 68
pulpit, xiii–xv, 1, 7, 20, 27, 32, 35–36, 38, 50, 54–55, 59, 64, 67–70, 72–74, 84, 86–93, 96, 107, 113, 122–23, 125–26
Purvis-Smith, Virginia, 126

race/racial, xii, 6, 38, 57, 62, 70n33, 113, 120
Rahab/Rahab's prism, 39
reason, 5, 68–69, 117, 120
reconciliation, 122–23
register, xiii, xv–xvii, 47–51, 54–55, 60, 67, 74–75, 77–78, 82–91, 94–95, 101, 107–8, 111–12, 115, 118, 123–25, 129, 133
revelation, 21–22, 46, 77, 93
rhetoric/rhetorical, 30, 50, 87, 104, 107n26
Roundtable Pulpit, 125
Roman Catholic, xvi, 85, 111–13
Ruether, Rosemary Radford, 2n2, 46, 71, 97n2

sacrament, 5, 11, 15, 20, 26, 114
sacramental imagination, 112–13
same-sex, 37, 44, 53
Samaritan woman, 6
sanctification, 109
Schüssler Fiorenza, Elizabeth, 2n2, 46, 76
scripture, xiii–xv, 3, 9, 13–14, 21–22, 27, 30, 32, 45–46, 51–53, 64, 68, 75–76, 92–93, 108–10, 113, 116–17, 119–20, 125, 128, 133
Second Great Awakening, 109
sermon, xii–xvi, 3, 7, 14, 24, 26–31, 33–35, 43, 46–47, 49–55, 60, 63–64, 66–68, 71, 73, 75–79, 81, 83–90, 92, 94–99, 101–8, 110–15, 117, 119–20, 122–24, 127–28, 131
Sermon on the Mount, 3
sex, xii, 6, 11, 22, 81, 110, 132n15
sexes, 6
sexism, 45, 57
sexual, 15, 61
  abstinence, 12
  activity, 4, 11, 15
  behavior, xii
  binaries, 71
  difference, xii, 72
  dimorphism, xii
  identification, 29
  orientation, 38, 62
  practice, 11, 44
  purity, 12–13, 15, 22
  status, 15
sexuality, xii, 13, 43–45, 76, 87, 116
sexy, 88
Small Catechism, 41
Smith, Christine, xvi, 96–102, 127
social location, 50, 55, 83, 118
Solomon, 120
soul, 46, 69–70, 104
Southern Baptist Convention, 26n1, 59
standpoint/standpoint theory, 55–58, 96, 101, 110, 124
Stephen, 11
suffrage, 62
Synoptic Gospels, 18

Tanner, Kathryn, 37
temptation, 88
testify/testimony, xii, 1, 25, 32, 52, 68, 100, 103–4, 108–11, 125, 130
Thecla, 12–13
tradition, xi–xii, xv–xvi, 17–18, 22, 35–38, 40–41, 43, 45, 51, 53, 55–56, 76–77, 85, 91, 93, 96, 102, 111–12, 117, 120
  academic, 40

147

Name and Subject Index

tradition (*continued*)
  biblical, xv, 14, 76
  Christian, 19, 45, 114
  church, 2, 33, 75
  congregational, 97
  ecclesial, xv, 21, 29, 102
  Jesus, 16
  Johannine, 18
  oral, 17
  theological, 97
transcendence/transcendent, xiv, 41, 68, 70, 112, 126–27, 131
transsexual, 40
Tubman, Harriett, 38–39

United Methodist Church, 25n1, 64n26, 124n4

Vashti, 104–5
violence, 44
virgins, 7, 11–12, 15, 20, 57
voice

Weeks, Kathi, 56–60, 101, 105, 126
Wesley, John, 1, 24–25
Whitehead, Mary Beth, 121, 121n61
widows, 6–7, 11–12, 15, 57
witness, xii, 3, 13–14, 19, 22–23, 26, 32–33, 36, 108, 115, 132
wives, 12
Wollstonecraft, Mary, 61–63, 133
woman, xii–xiii, 4–6, 8–10, 21, 23–24, 27–29, 31, 33–36, 38n24, 43, 50, 55–56, 59–61, 63–74, 80–83, 85–86, 88, 90–92, 94–95, 97, 105, 108–9, 113, 120, 123–24, 126, 130–32
womanhood, 4
women, xi–xii, xiv–xvii, 1–27, 29–35, 38–46, 50, 53, 55–68, 70–77, 82–83, 85–86, 88, 90–113, 118, 122–25, 127–28, 131, 132n15
  AICs, 40
  authority of, xv, 16, 18, 21
  biblical, 46
  clergy, 102
  clergy rights, 93
  construct, 86
  contributions of, xiii, xv, 21, 29, 62, 65
  distinctiveness of, 30, 35, 70, 72, 131
  equality, 57, 62
  exclusion of, 22, 24, 71, 77, 89
  experiences, xiv, 59, 93, 95–97, 133
  image of, 65
  inclusion of, 25, 76, 89
  independence of, 12
  leadership, 2, 9, 17–18
  legitimacy of, 82
  lives of, 55, 59, 100, 115
  middleclass, 43
  perspective of, 24
  practices of, 66
  preachers, xiv, 2, 27, 30, 34, 48, 58–59, 61, 70, 83, 91, 111, 123, 132–33
  preaching, 48, 95, 103, 118, 122–23
  presence of, 45, 65, 125
  privileged, 43
  proclamation, 75, 103
  oppression, 55–56, 76
  ordination, 111
  role of, 4, 15, 17, 23–25, 76
  scripting of, xv, 63
  sinfulness, 99
  speech, 42
  status of, 8
  subjugated, 108
  submission of, xv
  subordination of, xv
  suffrage, 62
  testimony, xii, 1, 109
  upper- class, 56
  value of, 115
  voices, xi–xiii, xvi, 22, 32, 34, 45–47, 49, 62, 75, 102–3, 108, 111, 113, 117, 123–26
  white, 43
  witness, xii ,13–14
  words of, 104, 110–11
  work of, 15, 25, 43, 56, 59, 112
  working class, 56
Women in the Pulpit Sunday, 64

Scripture Index

Exodus
1:15–21   57
2   110–11

Ruth
                 xvn10

I Samuel
                 xvn10

II Samuel
                 xvn10

I Kings
3:16–28   120
19:12   94

Esther
                 104–5

Isaiah
9   115

Jeremiah
32:15   131

Matthew
10:36   12

15:21–18   39

Luke
1:26–38   104
1:38   123
15:1–10   33
15:3–7   33
15:8–10   33

John
1:46   89
3:1–10   79
20:6–9   18
20:18   1
20:27   18

Acts
2:14   3
2:46   14
6:1   10
6:9   11
7:2   3
11:19   3
16:13   3
18:26   6n18

Romans
8:19   115
16:1–2   10
16:3–16   14
16:3–5   14
16:6   9

Scripture Index

I Corinthians

11:1	8
11:3	8
11:10	8
14:26	7
14:34	2, 82

II Corinthians

5:19	122

Galatians

3:27–28	6
3:28	2, 70

II Timothy

	9

Gospel of Mary

10:13	18
10:14	17

www.ingramcontent.com/pod-product-compliance
Lightning Source LLC
Chambersburg PA
CBHW030858170426
43193CB00009BA/658